*Sunset*

# ARRANGING
# flowers
## *from* *your* garden

BY CYNTHIA BIX, PHILIP EDINGER, AND THE EDITORS OF SUNSET BOOKS

MENLO PARK, CALIFORNIA

# THE KINDEST CUT

The beauty of flowers is uplifting, soul soothing. What could be more natural, then, than gathering flowers for enjoyment indoors? They can brighten a dreary day, revive the spirit with their freshness and fragrance, and transform a humdrum space into one of color and life. Whether you opt for a few snowdrops in a perfume bottle, a solitary camellia floating in a cut-glass bowl, a modest bunch of wildflowers, or a full-blown arrangement packed with countless kinds and hues of blossoms, there's a place for cut flowers in anyone's life. In these pages, we show just where those places are—from the kitchen windowsill to the festive holiday table, from the bathroom shelf to the grand living room mantelpiece. Styles run the gamut, too, from the almost stark simplicity of a few bare branches to the full-blown exuberance of lavish bouquets that recall Dutch floral still lifes.

As you look through this book, you'll also find advice on cutting and conditioning materials to give them the longest possible vase life. You'll learn some standard techniques for putting arrangements together; you'll meet a variety of plants that are favorites for cutting. And we've devoted a full chapter to gardening basics—techniques and tips to help you plant and care for flowers for cutting, including a sampler of designs for beautiful cutting gardens.

We are deeply grateful to the following contributors for their invaluable assistance and advice: Barbara Erfani, *Erfani Floral Studio,* Berkeley, California; Karen Taddei, *Lilacs Floral Design,* Marstons Mills, Massachusetts; Lyn Williams, Sharon Schwartz, and Marcia Pleas, *Brown & Greene Floral Market,* Minneapolis, Minnesota; and *Magic Gardens,* Berkeley, California.

## SUNSET BOOKS INC.

Vice President, General Manager: Richard A. Smeby
Vice President, Editorial Director: Bob Doyle
Production Director: Lory Day
Director of Operations: Rosann Sutherland
Art Director: Vasken Guiragossian

**Staff for this book:**

Managing Editor: Marianne Lipanovich
Copy Editor: Rebecca LaBrum
Photo Director/Stylist: JoAnn Masaoka Van Atta
Principal Photographers: Scott Atkinson, E. Andrew McKinney
Contributing Editor: Tom Wilhite
Proofreader: Suzanne Normand Eyre
Indexer: Nanette Cardon
Production Coordinator: Eligio Hernandez

Art Director: Alice Rogers
Garden Illustrator: Jenny Speckels
Gardening Technique Illustrator: Erin O'Toole
Garden Designs: Philip Edinger
Computer Production: Linda Bouchard

*Cover: Photograph by Scott Atkinson.*
*Photo styling by JoAnn Masaoka Van Atta.*

## PHOTOGRAPHERS:

**All-America Rose Selection:** 109 top right; **Jean Allsopp:** 53 bottom right, 72 top, 77; **Curtis Anderson:** 75 bottom; **Scott Atkinson:** 1, 2, 3 top, middle left, 4–5. 22 bottom left, bottom middle, bottom right, 23 bottom left, bottom middle, bottom right, 27 bottom, 32, 33, 35 bottom right, 36–37, 38, 39 bottom, 41 bottom left, 42, 43 top, 44, 54 bottom left, bottom right, 46, 47 top, 51 bottom, 52, 53 top, bottom left, 54, 55, 56 top, 57, 58, 59, 60 top, bottom left, 62, 62, 63, 64, 65, 70, 71, 78, 90, 99; **Noel Barnhurst:** 74, 75 top; **Marion Brenner:** 69 bottom; **Karen Bussolini:** 82 right; **James Carrier:** 8 top right, 76 bottom; **David Cavagnaro:** 80 top; **Rosalind Creasy:** 25 middle, 30 top; **Stephen Cridland:** 82 left; **Claire Curran:** 20 bottom, 60 bottom right, 67 bottom, 79, 108 bottom; **Robin Cushman:** 9 top; **R. Todd Davis:** 39 top right; **Alan & Linda Detrick:** 16 bottom left, 18, 19 bottom right, 20 top, 21, 26, 28 top, 29 bottom left, 31 top, 69 top; **Derek Fell:** 104; **Roger Foley:** 15 top; **Andy Freeburg:** 11 top; **David Goldberg:** 50 bottom, 81 bottom right; **Ken Gutmaker:** 16 top; **Jamie Hadley:** 34, 35 bottom left, 73 top; **Philip Harvey:** 15 bottom, 25 bottom left, 35 top, 43 bottom, 98; **Saxon Holt:** 3 middle right, 7 top, 8 top left, bottom, 10 bottom, 12–13, 22 top, 29 top, 91; **Lee Valley Garden Tools:** 103 top; **Erich Lessig/Art Resource:** 28 bottom; **Barry Lewis:** 24 top left, top right, bottom right; **Renee Lynn:** 97; **Charles Mann:** 81 top, 95 bottom, 111 top; **Ells Marugg:** 109 bottom right; **Jack McDowell:** 109 middle right; **E. Andrew McKinney:** 14 top, 17 bottom, 23 top, 24 bottom left, 29 bottom right, 39 bottom left, 40, 41 top right, 45 top, 76 top, 84 top, bottom right, 85 top, 86, 87, 88, 89, 126, 127; **Kevin Miller:** 110; **Jerry Pavia:** 51 top, 56 bottom, 94, 96 bottom; **Norman A. Plate:** 3 bottom, 7 bottom, 19 top left, bottom right, 47 bottom, 72 bottom, 80 bottom, 83 top, bottom left, 92–93, 100, 106, 107, 108 top, 111 bottom, 112, 113; **Eric Roth:** 31 bottom; **Susan A. Roth:** 6 top, 17 top, 19 top left, 66, 95 top; **Sibila Savage:** 11 bottom, 27 top, 48, 49 bottom, 68 top, 83 bottom right; **Michael Skott:** 10 top, 14 bottom, 16 bottom right, 17 middle, 25 top, 30 bottom; **Michael S. Thompson:** 41 top left, 49 top, 50 top, 67 top, 81 bottom left, 96 middle, 109 top left; **Darrow M. Watt:** 103 bottom; **Tom Woodward:** 68 bottom, 73 bottom, 84 bottom left, 85 bottom; **Cynthia Woodyard:** 96 top; **Tom Wyatt:** 109 middle left, bottom left.

## FLORAL DESIGNS:

**Valerie Arelt:** 74–75; **Kim Haworth:** 73; **Gail Jacobs:** 15 top; **Louise Mercer:** 17 top, 19 top right; **Ellen Spector Platt:** 16 bottom left, 18, 19 bottom left, 20 top, 21, 26 top left, top right, 28 top, 29 bottom left, 31; **Bud Stuckey:** 19 bottom left.

# Contents

*Whether blooming out of doors or gracing the rooms in your home, flowers seem to make life better—more colorful, more pleasant, more serene. As a gardener or a garden lover,*

# FRESH FROM THE
# GARDEN

*you enjoy the way flowers combine with their surroundings. You step back and see them as one facet of a larger picture, a living landscape painting that includes the sky, green trees and lawns, and fences or house walls of wood, brick, or stone. When you bring the same blooms indoors, though, you enjoy them in a different way. A bouquet in a vase is like a still life. You tend to look closely, savoring the blossoms' special qualities: their colors and textures, even the shapes of their stems.*

*In the next few pages, we present a photographic celebration of the beauties of flowers, both indoors and out. Next, turn to Chapter 2, where you'll find help with every aspect of designing with flowers, from choosing the right vase to placing arrangements effectively in your rooms. In Chapter 3, we show you gorgeous arrangements to create in every season; you'll also find lists of the best flowers for cutting. Finally, Chapter 4 gives details on growing, harvesting, and even drying flowers, and provides inspiring plans for cut-flower gardens.*

Freshly picked from garden beds and borders, this lush collection of lilacs, delphiniums, bellflowers, tulips, and fluffy viburnum is ready to bring indoors.

**SHOWSTOPPERS** Taking a bow at the foyer mirror, this full-blown mixed bouquet (right) gains extra dazzle from its own reflection. Tulips, dogwood, and bleeding heart are enhanced with spiraea and kerria branches. Almost as eye-catching is a strikingly simple arrangement of just two vivid Iceland poppies (below).

# BOUQUETS ON STAGE
## PRESENTING SOLO STARS AND COLORFUL CHORUSES

*When beautifully arranged, almost any kind of flower has star potential—whether it performs solo, as a single, perfect stem in its own vase, or joins a bright chorus of other blossoms.*

**DELIGHTFUL DUOS** Bouquets featuring only two kinds of flowers—perhaps with a third type added for spice—are long-running favorites among arrangers. And when the partners are well-loved blooms like roses or hydrangeas, success is assured. At right, cream-colored roses and purple agapanthus form a closely packed dome inspired by the European pavé bouquet style. Below, mophead hydrangeas in soft hues cluster around stalks of 'Hopley's' oregano and wands of pink honeysuckle; ivy trails below. In both arrangements, the containers play perfect supporting roles.

# ALL THE GARDEN'S A STAGE
## WHERE THE FULL CAST TAKES A BOW

*Every successful production relies on a talented cast. In that vein, you might think of a cutting garden as providing the pool of players for your bouquets: floral "actors" that perform as beautifully on the big, outdoor stage as they do at smaller, more intimate venues indoors.*

**READY FOR THEIR CLOSE-UP** *Above:* Aspiring ensemble players wait in the wings for the floral director's arrangement. Brassy sunflowers consort with stately delphiniums, attended by a clutch of snapdragons. *Right:* A crowd of clamoring dahlias, ready for the picking.

**ANYTHING GOES** Mix styles, colors, sizes—your cutting garden doesn't have to follow a script. Here, a rustic sideyard planting effervesces with material for arrangements, from country-garden staples like yarrow, bee balm, and purple coneflower to sophisticated delphiniums.

9

# ROOMS IN BLOOM
## ENHANCING YOUR HOME
## WITH FLOWERS

*Every room in the house comes alive when you fill it with flowers. A large, dramatic bouquet can be the focal point of a room; a small, understated one can be a subtle surprise. Large or small, bold or dainty, in a group or standing alone, bouquets of blooms say, "Welcome."*

**PLACES FOR VASES**  The place for flowers in your home is... anywhere. A fireplace mantel (facing page, top) is a natural stage for a trio of simple bouquets in pastel ceramic vases; the corner of a sink (facing page, bottom) is a not-so-obvious but equally appropriate spot. In any room, a tall arrangement like the flowering quince shown above supplies an instant focal point and conversation piece.

DESIGNING WITH

# FLOWERS

*Bringing the beauty of blossoms and foliage from your garden into your home doubles the rewards of growing flowers. You get to enjoy the sights, scents, and colors of your borders and beds any day, any time, anywhere in the house. A bouquet of cream-and-pink roses gathered at the peak of perfection lends an atmosphere of luxury and romance to a bedroom; a single jaunty sunflower on the kitchen table perks up a family supper. Gracing the sideboard in the dining room, an elegant assembly of gloriosa daisies, brilliant cotoneaster berries, and oak leaves proclaims abundance and hospitality.*

*Successful flower arranging is an art that anyone can learn. As a garden lover, you already have one important requirement: appreciation of your flowers' form, texture, and color. Combine that with a sense of style in your choice of containers, a spirit of fun and imagination when placing arrangements in your rooms, and a little know-how regarding the tools and techniques floral designers use—and you're assured of success. In this chapter, you'll find all the advice and information you need, including inspiring photographs, to set you on your way toward filling your home with beautiful arrangements of all your favorite flowers.*

A beautifully orchestrated composition of flowers, vase, and wallpaper
lends vibrant color and life to this room.

# FLOWER-FILLED ROOMS

*Bring fresh flowers indoors, and a kind of magic happens. From casual den to elegant dining area, any room in the house comes to life with the colors and scents of the garden. And if you've grown the flowers yourself, there's a feeling of connection with something lovingly nurtured and carefully chosen that adds an extra, personal dimension to the experience.*

STYLE. The best marriages of rooms and floral arrangements are based on "reading" the ambience and style of a room and using flowers to enhance both. It helps to think of the flowers and their containers as part and parcel of your decor, just like the wallpaper, window treatments, floor coverings, and upholstery. Flowers and container together form a decorative unit that should echo the room's mood and style. For example, a formal living room with high ceilings, large windows, and elegant furni-

ture is just the right setting for a bouquet of flawless roses, perhaps displayed in an antique Chinese ginger jar. At the opposite end of the style spectrum, a casual sun porch with white beadboard walls, scattered with a friendly mix of flea-market tables and garden chairs, would be an ideal spot for a galvanized tub filled with sunflowers and brilliant zinnias. In a contemporary space, where sparse, clean-lined furnishings and an expanse of tinted concrete floor bespeak a minimalist sensibility, a handcrafted glass art piece holding carefully selected branches of curly-leafed willow or tall, sculptural alliums might make a stunning focal point.

Because your home's interior and your garden are already expressions of your taste, the flowers you bring indoors will probably be natural matches for your decor. If you're unsure about what's appropriate in a particular room, look at photos in magazines and decorating books for inspiration. You'll probably see plenty of rooms that share characteristics with yours, and these are likely to be pictured with flower and foliage arrangements that enhance that style of room.

COLOR. The colors in your flower arrangements should be as personal as those you've chosen for curtains, carpeting, or sofa. In your garden, you have doubtless assembled a living palette of favorite flowers in the colors you love, and these will form the backbone for your arrangements. Of course, the available palette changes with the seasons, expanding your choices throughout the year and allowing you to vary the feel of your rooms as the months go by.

In any case, you can't go wrong in choosing flowers that match or complement a room's color scheme or dominant colors—those of wallpaper and paint, upholstery, window treatments, and so on. Another approach is to pick up or complement the colors of objects in the room, such as decorative glass or ceramic pieces or a particular painting. When you're selecting flowers for a dining table or buffet, the dishes may provide the color cue. A table set with green-sprigged bone china might look lovely with a fresh centerpiece of green bells-of-Ireland or lady's-mantle combined with pure white Shasta daisies and strands of needlepoint ivy.

Generally speaking, arrangements in vibrant hues look best in rooms with a fairly neutral scheme, whereas a colorful, very "busy" room might benefit from flowers in a single color or perhaps even an all-green foliage arrangement. Of course, rules are made to be broken, and you may have great success with pairings that are just the opposite of these examples.

ABOVE: Centered on a gleaming glass table, a spherical vase holding a sculptural arrangement of dogwoods and magenta tulips makes a bold, contemporary statement.

LEFT: Elegance and symmetry characterize this boudoir dressing table. The luxury of the satin skirt, silver and gold accessories, and matching lamps calls for a simple yet elegant pair of arrangements —such as two clear glass vases of pink tulips.

FACING PAGE, TOP: Two arrangements—an all-of-a-kind display of long-stemmed apricot tulips and an extravagant mixed bouquet that combines the same tulips with companion flowers—play up this lovely room's grand proportions and sunny palette.

FACING PAGE, BOTTOM: A jaunty mantelpiece grouping of sunflowers, partnered with shiny green apples and a delightful folk-art piece, strikes just the right note of country charm.

SIZE AND SCALE. Where you locate your arrangement will play an important role in determining its size, its scale (that is, its size in relation to other elements in the room), and its character. Common sense will help you out here: small or low-ceilinged rooms typically look best with bouquets that are fairly small and dainty, while large, airy spaces call for something tall and imposing.

Bear in mind, though, that even an open area may have intimate corners that suit smaller-scale arrangements. A romantic bedroom—perhaps a confection of gauzy white curtains and peaches-and-cream bed linens—features an old-fashioned dressing table that's the perfect place for an etched-glass bowl of apricot roses and maidenhair fern. A sunny kitchen centered around a scrubbed pine table has a deep windowsill that makes an ideal perch for a row of colorful mismatched ceramic cups, each sporting a stem or two of marigolds. Small-scale arrangements such as these have their greatest appeal when viewed at close range. The boudoir's roses are positioned right where you can appreciate their scent and beauty as you sit at the dressing table; the kitchen windowsill is over the sink, letting you enjoy the flowers' cheery color as you work.

In contrast, an arrangement placed in a showcase position—on a mantel, for instance, as shown at left—is best appreciated from across the room. This usually calls for more drama in form and flower choice; you will probably use either a single, dramatic vase bearing a large-scale arrangement, or a grouping of smaller bouquets that together create a lavish, full effect.

Dining-table centerpieces present a special challenge. They must look striking when seen from a distance—as guests enter the room—and be appealing from close up, as well. They must also leave ample room for place settings and serving pieces, and be low enough to let diners chat across the table without having to peer around the arrangement. For this reason, such arrangements are often assembled in low bowls or pans. But you do have other options. For instance, you might march a row of identical small vases, each holding

just one or two blooms, down the center of the table. The number of containers makes the display showy from far off, while their dainty individual size makes for a pleasing view close up.

CREATIVE USES—AND PLACES—FOR ARRANGEMENTS. As we've just discussed, a flower arrangement has something to offer almost any room. Be creative with the impression you want to make—and use your imagination in placing the arrangement, too. Most people tend to choose a few key rooms (dining room, living room, bedroom) and a few key spots: on hall and entryway or foyer tables, mantels, coffee tables, buffets, dining tables. But keep other locations in mind, as well.

- Place an arrangement in front of a favorite painting to enhance the painting's colors and textures.

- Create a sense of order and symmetry by placing matching arrangements on either side of a fireplace or doorway, or on two matching end tables.

- Set an arrangement in front of a mirror—you'll magically double the floral abundance.

- On a mantel or a long table, line up a row of identical small vases with identical single blossoms; alternate them with votive candles in pretty coordinating candleholders, if you like. (When you see a collection of small, inexpensive vases, buy several to use this way.)

- On a table featuring objets d'art, collectibles, or books, add a floral arrangement to bring a touch of the garden to the tableau; use contrasts in texture and color to add interest.

- Create a grouping of vases and other containers, some filled with flowers and some empty.

- Line a windowsill with a collection of mismatched bottles and small vases bearing seasonal cuttings (but take care that blossoms aren't overexposed to sun).

- To dramatize an empty corner—in an entryway, by a stairway—place an oil jar or other large container on the floor and fill it with tall cut branches, either bare ones or those of spring-flowering trees or shrubs.

- Liven up a bookshelf or other display shelf by adding a floral arrangement in an appropriate space.

- Encourage sweet dreams with a modest arrangement on a bedside table. Make sure you use a small, well-balanced vase, placed in a spot where it won't be knocked over in a grope for the water carafe in the wee hours or wild grab for the alarm clock in the morning!

- Perk up your home office and/or desk, or even your workshop table or laundry room, with a casual arrangement. It will do wonders for your spirits when the work gets difficult or tedious.

- Place an informal arrangement of flowers and/or foliage on your kitchen work table, counter, or windowsill.

- Surprise someone with a miniature vase holding just one or two blooms on a bed tray or alongside the plate at an everyday meal.

- Put a bright arrangement of cheerful flowers like miniature sunflowers or pert-faced pansies in your children's rooms (make sure the vase is low and stable).

- Sweeten the bath area with a small, fresh-looking arrangement on the vanity, toilet tank, or tub surround.

- Change the look of a room seasonally with a rotating display of flowers in the same spot.

- Give a neutral room an instant lift with a blast of color from a dynamic plant-vase combination.

# THE NATURE OF FLOWERS

*As a garden lover, you already have a keen appreciation for the endlessly beautiful and interesting forms and colors of flowers and foliage. You've laid out your garden beds to take these factors into account, thinking about how each plant best combines with its fellows. The same principles apply to creating successful flower arrangements.*

SEASONAL FLOWER COLOR. Throughout the year, your garden probably displays a general pattern of seasonal color. When you cut the flowers, you'll automatically bring in a particular palette that will provide an indoor reflection of the beauties outside. And of course, your floral arrangements will also reflect your personal preference in colors and color combinations.

PERENNIAL GREENS  In all seasons, even the smallest garden boasts something green. In winter, this color may be found only in evergreens, but in every other season it's at hand in the foliage of countless plants—and even in some blossoms. Far from being monotonal, the garden's greens display an infinite range, from vivid chartreuse to glossy deep green to soft, silvery near-gray. Though green foliage in all its variety enhances many flowers, it's also beautiful on its own. And don't overlook arrangements of green or green-tinged flowers, such as snowball viburnum, hellebore, and bells-of-Ireland.

**SPRING'S FRESH COLORS**
As winter ends and new growth begins, your garden reveals its charms gradually, with colors that echo the season's sunshine, blue skies, and billowing white clouds. Spring brings the soft yellows, creams, and whites of early-blooming bulbs, as well as blues and purples that vary from delicate to intense. The whites and soft to vivid pinks of flowering trees and shrubs add another stroke to the season's fresh palette.

**SUMMER'S SIZZLERS** With the coming of summer, the garden becomes a brilliant carnival of color. As one flower after another bursts into bloom, a palette featuring every color under the sun emerges—along with fresh white and many shades of green from foliage. Whether you revel in a bold mix or prefer to focus on just two or three central colors, a multitude of choices is available in this season of vigorous growth.

**AUTUMN'S RICHES** Russets, golds, tawny oranges, rich browns, vivid scarlets—these are the colors of autumn, found in flowers like chrysanthemums, dahlias, and sunflowers as well as in berries, seedpods, and changing leaves. Warm, mellow hues glow in the garden and on every shrub and tree, and they're the backbone of arrangements for Thanksgiving tables and fireplace mantelpieces.

**WINTER'S CONTRASTS** The winter garden offers subtle colors and surprising contrasts. In mild-winter regions, evergreen foliage hues are enlivened by strokes of white and surprise bursts of color —in flowers like winter-blooming camellias and bright fruits such as persimmons. Where winters are cold, gardens gain drama from the stark lines of bare, dark branches against white snow, accented by the deep greens of conifers and occasional bright berries.

**SPRING'S FRESH COLORS**

**SUMMER'S SIZZLERS**

**AUTUMN'S RICHES**

**WINTER'S CONTRASTS**

USING AND COMBINING COLOR. When you choose colors for a floral arrangement, keep in mind that the arrangement should complement its surroundings—usually the color scheme of the room in which it will be displayed. It may either blend with and enhance those colors or provide a dramatic contrast that will make it an exciting focal point.

In creating the arrangement itself, you can take one of two main approaches. With the *monochromatic* approach, you focus on one color. You can use flowers of a single color—all intense purple violets, for example, or all golden yellow chrysanthemums. Or you can choose flowers in different values of a color; for example, combine roses in gradations of pink, from deep cerise to very light, delicate blush pink. Often, varieties of a single species have blossoms in related colors that blend naturally.

With the *combined* approach, you mix different colors. You can put together *harmonizing,* or closely related, colors, such as red, pink, and orange. To keep the bouquet from looking dull, vary the colors' values. For example, combine deep red dahlias, hot pink zinnias, and pastel apricot lilies; the brightness of the dahlias and zinnias enlivens the softness of the lilies. Another way to combine colors is to mix blooms in *contrasting* hues, such as orange and blue or yellow and violet. This approach can be a bit tricky, but when done well, it has dramatic and eye-catching results, especially if you combine two intense colors—vivid orange parrot tulips and deep blue hyacinths, for example. For a softer contrast, try lighter values of the basic colors: pair creamy apricot tulips with ice blue hyacinths. Or use blossoms with differing values (one light, one dark), such as pale peach roses and bright blue hydrangeas. The total effect is also determined by the amount of each color you use; try combining them in unequal amounts, letting one serve as an accent to greater amounts of the other.

The impression your arrangement makes will depend partly on the *intensity* of the colors you use. For a bold statement, choose jewel tones, such as deep, rich blue, violet,

ABOVE: Delphiniums and larkspur bloom in a range of naturally harmonious colors.

RIGHT: A mixed bouquet of roses, columbine, and Jupiter's beard in various pink shades illustrates the use of harmonizing colors. White feverfew, along with green maidenhair fern and other foliage, gives the arrangement balance.

FACING PAGE, TOP: Casual bunches of various flowers pack plenty of color punch. The harmonious reds, oranges, and yellows of poppies, daylilies, butterfly weed, and blanket flower contrast dramatically with the brilliant blue of the bachelor's buttons in the arrangement's center.

FACING PAGE, BOTTOM: For a show-stopping bouquet, a lush bunch of tulips in intense jewel tones of warm pink and red is sparked with a few yellow daffodils.

and red (see page 44 for an example). For a softer look, choose lighter, less saturated pastel and neutral shades such as peach, cream, lavender, and the like. For unexpected drama, place a bit of contrasting color in an arrangement of harmonizing flowers—add a few shocking yellow Dutch irises to a vase filled with violet and blue lilacs and hyacinths, for example.

When mixing several colors, intersperse green or gray foliage or white flowers as "peacemakers" to create overall harmony. Green is especially effective for pulling together contrasting colors and also acts as a foil for brighter ones. Moreover, most shades of green, from the apple green of bells-of-Ireland to the dark green of ivy, blend harmoniously with one another. And white—whether from Shasta daisies, stock, or baby's breath—always adds sparkle and freshness.

When you combine colors, keep in mind that they may be either *warm* or *cool.* Warm colors—yellows, oranges, and yellow-based reds and greens—appear to advance when you look at them, while cool colors—blues, violets, and blue-based reds and greens—seem to recede. Juxtaposing warm and cool colors in an arrangement makes each look more intense, whereas keeping to all-warm or all-cool hues results in a more blended look. But beware of placing cool-color bouquets in rooms with low light; the arrangement may fade into obscurity unless you brighten it by adding white flowers.

FLOWER FORM AND TEXTURE. From the fluffy pouf of a hydrangea head to the thistly dome of an artichoke blossom, from the tall, upright spire of a delphinium stalk to the softly nodding bell of a snowdrop—every flower has a unique character, expressed in the shape, color, and texture of its blossoms and leaves and even in the nature of its stem. Usually, a flower or plant's form and growth habit will suggest the best way to use it in an arrangement. Following are examples of how various flowers lend themselves to particular treatments.

- **Tall flower spikes** Flowers such as delphiniums, gladioli, and foxgloves feature multiple flowers growing along tall, strong stems. Dramatic and elegant, flowers like these make stunning all-of-a-kind bouquets. But with careful selection, such stems can also be used as the backbone of an arrangement in which various flower forms are mixed.

- **Fluffy flower heads** These are the can't-miss choices for arrangers. They include favorites such as hydrangeas, lilacs, and snowball viburnum, which feature lush, full clusters of many tiny flowers. An armful of these is all you need to make a truly lavish bouquet, but you can also combine a few of them with foliage or other flowers to fill out an arrangement instantly.

- **Showy flowers on upright stems** This very general category includes the aristocrats of the cut-flower world, such as roses and lilies, as well as old-fashioned favorites like sunflowers. They have in common showy flower heads atop stems sturdy enough to hold them up proudly. They offer a staggering variety of forms and textures, from the velvety rose to the spiky dahlia, from the saucerlike sunflower to the elegant, trumpet-shaped Asiatic lily. These are often the showpieces of an arrangement, whether massed in an all-of-a-kind bouquet or mixed with other flowers. You can sometimes give them quite different looks, depending on how long or short you cut their stems. Some designers feel that like-textured flowers—such as many-petaled zinnias, dahlias, and chrysanthemums, or silky-smooth roses and lilies—belong together. Others like to mix textures. Take your pick!

## COMBINING FLOWER FORMS

It's possible to make beautiful arrangements using only one or two flower types. But if you want to create an arrangement incorporating some of each of the types described on these two pages (except the very short-stemmed ones), begin by placing the tall, spiky flower stalks first, to establish the arrangement's height and line. The showy focal point–type flowers or the fluffy, rounded types, cut to a medium height, are inserted next, either in bundles or individually. After this, you can add soft-stemmed flowers and let them droop over the container's neck; alternatively, you can insert them in such a way that the other, sturdier flowers hold them more upright. Next comes a small amount of filler; finally, insert any trailing or vine-like material around the edges. The general idea is to create a smoothly graduated look, without any gaps that cause the eye to jump over empty space. For more specific arranging techniques and approaches, see pages 28–33.

Tall flower spike
(foxglove)

Fluffy flower head
(hydrangea)

Showy flower
(lily)

- **Flowers with soft or curving stems** These feature handsome blossoms on individual stems that are curved and/or a bit on the soft or floppy side. Some, like tulips, have stems that naturally curve gently as they age, so that the blooms eventually nod on the stem ends. Others, like ranunculus or poppies, have stems that are always curvy; still others, like sweet peas, have very soft, weak stems. You can combine these types of flowers with more upright flowers and foliage and let them hang gracefully over the lip of the container; or, to get them to stand more upright, cluster them densely in a narrow-necked vase.

- **Cloudlike filler plants** Favorites such as lady's-mantle, baby's breath, love-in-a-mist, and some heaths and heathers fall into this category. With their typically dainty foliage and many small stems scattered with tiny flowers, these fine-textured plants have a light, airy look. Use them alone or as fillers in a bouquet, to lend a look of softness and fullness. But don't use too much—just enough to frame and complement dramatic individual flowers such as peonies, dahlias, and the like.

- **Short-stemmed flowers** Some of these flowers, such as magnolias and camellias, have such short stems that, unless you use the branch on which they grow, you cannot really put them in a vase. These lovely blooms are often best displayed floating in a shallow container of water, where their color and structure can be appreciated. Others, like pansies or lily-of-the-valley, are charming when displayed in tiny glasses or other containers.

- **Trailing plants** Flowering vines provide a delightful addition to many mixed arrangements. Morning glories, jasmine, honeysuckle, potato vine, and passion flowers can be tucked into the edges of an arrangement and allowed to trail down the side of the container and even along the table or mantel. Their nonflowering counterparts, the ivies, also add a nice touch, either as greenery or, in some cases (Boston ivy, for example), autumn color.

Short-stemmed flower
(magnolia)

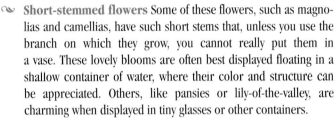

Flower with curving stem
(tulip)

Cloudlike filler
(Queen Anne's lace)

Trailing plant
(ivy)

# BEAUTIFUL CONTAINERS

*In any arrangement, the flowers are only half the picture. The container is of equal importance, helping to set the tone of an arrangement and connect it to its surroundings. A container's material gives it its basic style. Gleaming silver and fine porcelain are naturally elegant, for example, while galvanized metal and rough-textured, earthy pottery are inherently casual and countrified.*

COLOR AND PATTERN. A container may echo a room's patterns and colors in various ways. In a sitting room with chairs upholstered in flowered rose-and-pink chintz, for instance, you might choose a china vase with a pattern of pink roses and fill it with cream-colored tulips. In a room with lots of bright colors and interesting patterns, you might select a solid-colored ceramic pitcher in one of the hues and fill it with multicolored flowers. Going for contrast or accent is another possibility: the same bright ceramic pitcher could be a striking focal point in a room done in neutrals. And of course, clear glass containers can go almost anywhere.

The choice of container can also play up other aspects of the room. For a space flooded with natural light, you might select a large glass vase and fill it with long-stemmed white nerines—the light will make the water-filled vase sparkle and increase the brightness of the flowers.

CONTAINER MATERIALS. Gleaming silver, rustic pottery, tinted glass—you can choose from a huge variety of container materials. Following is a survey of the impressive array available.

*Glass.* Whether it takes the form of an antique cut-glass pitcher or a clean-lined contemporary vase, whether it's clear, translucent, or tinted, glass is always beautiful. It's also adaptable, complementing almost any arrangement and usually blending with any decor. In addition to vases, you can use a multitude of other glass items—anything goes! Try bottles, apothecary or canning jars, drinking glasses, bowls, pitchers, fishbowls—the list is limited only by your imagination.

Of course, a glass container lets you see the stems, so paying special attention to them gives arrangements in clear glass a wonderful added dimension. For example, a bunch of snapdragons, callas, or daffodils with stems cut to one length and gently twisted into a spiral (see page 38) is showy both above and below the water line.

With all glass containers, make sure to keep the water very clean; change it daily, if possible, so the view into and through the container will be crystal clear. And remember that a glass container is not the place to use mechanics that will show, such as metal frogs or floral foam.

Whether made from ceramic, silver, glass, or some other material, beautiful containers complete any floral arrangement.

*Silver.* The gleam of silver adds elegance and brightness, lifting flower arrangements to new heights of glamour. In addition to vases, try using bowls, serving dishes, cream pitchers, coffeepots, teapots, even mint julep cups. For best effect, the flowers you choose should be dramatic or lush enough to stand up to the lavish look of the silver.

*Copper, bronze, and other metals.* From the warm glow of an old copper kettle or elegant bronze bowl to the cool shine of a galvanized florist's bucket or watering can, metal pieces make unobtrusive yet complementary containers for many kinds of flowers. Dark metal sets off pale blossoms and lends richness to intense colors; tin and galvanized metal brighten almost any color. Metal is a slightly unusual container choice, and for that reason it's fun to work with. You can enjoy playing with unexpected contrasts; try filling a rustic galvanized tub with elegant peonies, for example. Note that while many galvanized containers are made to hold water, other metal pieces may require you to use a glass jar, plastic tub, or other liner to prevent rusting and leaking (see page 46).

THE MOST BEAUTIFUL FLOWERS

*Ceramic.* This broad category encompasses a great range of choices, from antique china to contemporary ceramics to rough earthenware. Among fine porcelain and china, you'll find everything from blue-and-white Chinese willowware to English Wedgwood and French Haviland to painted pieces from the Art Nouveau and Art Deco periods. Many vintage pieces are patterned rather than solid colored. Beautiful contemporary china, decorated with floral or geometric designs, is also an option.

The porcelain or china pieces you choose as containers typically aren't intended for use as vases; they may be pitchers, bowls, teapots, or anything else that will comfortably hold flowers. Of course, you must be careful not to scratch the insides with sharp cut branches; it may be necessary to cushion the bottom and sides of the piece with clear cellophane or plastic wrap before creating your arrangement.

Solid-colored ceramics are the easiest of all to use. They can be found in hues that complement most color schemes and flowers, they make a nice foil for mixed arrangements, and they are easy to group successfully. Old or new, such containers come in muted colors that let the flowers shine and in bright ones that make the container a

Creative choices in containers run the gamut from a weathered metal garden urn *(top)* to a vintage Fiesta ware pitcher *(middle)* to an elegantly glazed ceramic vase *(bottom)*.

showstopper all on its own. Some floral designers swear by all-white ceramic (English ironstone, for example). Many solid-colored ceramics, such as Bauer and vintage Fiesta ware, are highly collectible in their own right.

Earthenware or pottery, the country cousin of porcelain, is a natural for cut flowers. Glazed or unglazed, these pots, jugs, bowls, and jars look great in a casual setting, filled with an assortment of cottage-garden flowers. Or fill large earthenware containers with cut branches of trees and shrubs for a dramatic arrangement. Remember that porous, unglazed containers may leach moisture; place them in a saucer or tray to protect your furniture and floors.

*Basketry.* Thanks to their homespun texture and pleasing shapes, baskets are natural containers for flowers—especially for those with casual charm, like cosmos and sunflowers. Of course, you will need to use a liner of some kind for the water, such as a jam jar, plastic tub, or plastic bag (see page 42).

CONTAINER SIZE AND SHAPE. When you're selecting a container, always consider its size, relative both to the room and the flowers you'll be arranging. Large, dramatic flowers like gladioli and flowering tree branches usually require tall, generously proportioned vases (unless you cut the stems especially short). Smaller arrangements look best in smaller-scale containers, and very tiny flowers like violets and lily-of-the-valley call for petite holders like juice glasses or miniature bud vases.

The size and shape of the container will largely determine the size and shape of the arrangement it will hold. When you are relying on natural stems rather than on mechanics like floral foam and frogs (see pages 32–33), the single most important factor is the size of the container's neck relative to the numbers and types of flowers you are using. The neck should not be so wide that the flowers flop, nor should it be so narrow that they are crowded together or forced into an unnaturally upright position. You should also match the number of stems to the vase's size; if a vase is too large for the number of flowers, the arrangement will look skimpy. Finally, pay attention to the container's depth. It's usually best if the stems reach nearly to the bottom; that way, they won't be in danger of drying out if the water gets low before you have a chance to change it or top it up.

DESIGNER'S TIP Before you begin to arrange your flowers, place the empty vase or container where you want the finished arrangement to go—on your foyer table or mantel, for example. If the vase looks good and is in proportion to the room, the arrangement will look good.

## CHOOSING CONTAINER SHAPES

Below, we describe six basic container shapes and briefly discuss how they work with flowers. Containers in any of these shapes may be large or small, plain or fancy—and of course, each has many variations.

**FLARED OR TRUMPET SHAPED.** This container is narrower at the bottom than it is at the top, with a gracefully flared neck. The shape makes it easy to arrange natural-looking bouquets in which flower heads fan out in a full, rounded shape. A tall pitcher or classic tall, narrow urn works in much the same way.

**CYLINDER.** With the same narrow diameter from top to bottom, this versatile shape is useful for holding soft-stemmed flowers upright, for featuring a few dramatic flowers, or—if it's clear glass—for showing off stems twisted into an attractive pattern (see page 38). Be careful not to crowd a cylinder too tightly; the flowers will be crushed and/or look unnatural.

**GLOBE OR BUBBLE.** This attractive shape can be tricky to use. Most accommodating is a narrow-necked globe that lets flower stems spread below but controls them at the top. The rounded shape allows for beautiful, full-looking bouquets, but (as with the cylinder) be careful not to crowd in too many flowers.

**CUBE.** This square-necked container requires lots of flowers to look full. If you want to get away with fewer blooms, you can use mechanics inside the vase (see pages 32–33) or create an abstract, stylized look with a few flowers positioned at a slant. (For an imaginative use of small cubes, see page 53.)

**BOWL.** The low, wide bowl works best for floating flowers like camellias and magnolias. Some designers prefer footed bowls, which elevate the blossoms a bit for viewing. If you want to create arrangements in a bowl, you will have to use a frog, floral foam, or a tape grid (see pages 62–63).

**BOTTLE.** The very narrow neck of this container allows you to use only one or two stems: it's the perfect way to display a couple of beloved flowers. A grouping of bottles is especially attractive.

A pleasing combination of containers in different shapes makes for a decorative arrangement—even when you don't have many flowers to display.

Flared shapes

Bottles

Globes

Bowl

Cylinders

Cube

# CREATING FLOWER ARRANGEMENTS

*Over the centuries, styles of flower arranging have changed time and again. Approaches have ranged from the exuberant, informal floral extravaganzas of the Renaissance, as pictured in Dutch and Flemish still lifes, to the geometric arrangements—formal triangles, asymmetrical forms, and curves—of the early 20th century. And traditional Japanese flower arranging, or ikebana, has a unique elegant, linear style.*

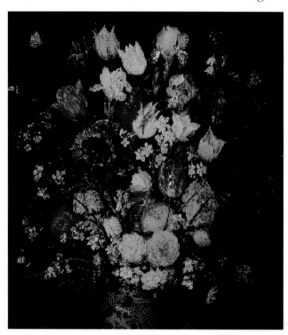

ABOVE: *Roses in a Blue Vase,* by the 17th-century Flemish artist Jan Bruegel the Elder.

ABOVE, RIGHT: A grouped arrangement shows off a collection of handsome tea and coffee pots; the interplay of various metals with the red tulips and purple grape hyacinths adds visual variety.

Today, many flower designers favor a natural approach that's perfect for the home gardener and flower arranger. Some even eschew mechanics such as frogs and floral foam, especially if these are intended to make the arrangement conform to a rigid geometric shape. Blossoms and other plant materials are more or less allowed to follow their own form and habit; they are supported by each other and by the neck of the container. The effect is unstructured and casual—though it can also be very sophisticated, depending on the container and the choice of flowers. In creating these arrangements, you follow your own aesthetic instincts rather than adhering to specific guidelines of the sort that applied to the highly formal designs of former times.

Of course, even a spontaneous-looking flower arrangement requires thought and care to create. And such arrangements do have an overall shape—determined partly by the container's form (see page 27) and partly by the growth habits of the flowers themselves. You can use both to create the look you want. Taken together, flowers and container may be dramatically tall and columnar; low and rounded; fan shaped; or even loosely triangular.

At times, you may need to use mechanics (see pages 32–33) to hold flowers in place, especially if you want to create a low table arrangement or one in a shallow bowl. Even in this case, though, you can follow the flowers' natural inclinations, so that the final creation has that informal appeal.

KINDS OF ARRANGEMENTS. Do you want to show off a single exquisite rose or fill a vase with dozens of the fragrant blooms? Or do you want variety, a riotous assortment of a half-dozen different kinds of flowers? All three options are popular with arrangers.

Many flowers look lovely when displayed individually. You might place a dramatic allium in a tall, narrow vase, float a perfect magnolia blossom in a crystal bowl, or show off a bright, fresh-faced pansy in an antique salt cellar. In every case, showcasing just one flower focuses the beholder's attention on its unique beauty and complexity. (When you treat a garden treasure in this way, pay special attention to scale, as described on page 16.)

The all-of-a-kind bouquet also celebrates the beauty of a particular kind of flower—but en masse, not singly. Choose whatever you love, be it roses or daffodils, daisies or lilacs, sweet peas or chrysanthemums. Such arrangements look particularly lavish, especially when they hold lots and lots of flowers (you may want to include some of the foliage, as well). You can create a layered look by varying the lengths of the stems, or you can leave them all the same length for a lush, massed look. You'll find a number of all-one-kind bouquets in this book; for just a few examples, see pages 45, 56, and 85.

If you love variety, the mixed bouquet is for you. The classic way to combine various kinds of flowers and foliage, this arrangement can take many forms: full-blown bouquets including many flower types (like the arrangement at right), very casual combinations of just a few favorite flowers, foliage arrangements accented with blossoms and berries. Examples of mixed bouquets appear throughout this book.

ONE VASE OR MANY? The most common arrangement is probably one in a single vase or other container, meant to be displayed all on its own. Sometimes, though, you'll opt for matching or coordinating arrangements in a pair of containers, such as bunches of daffodils at either end of a sideboard, or a nosegay of nasturtiums and Transvaal daisies beside each plate at a table set for two. And don't overlook arrangements that use several containers. These are lots of fun to create—you can let your imagination go! Do anything, from lining up a row of mismatched antique bottles of cuttings along a windowsill to clustering a group of all-one-color ceramic vases on a sideboard, then filling some with small bouquets and leaving some empty. Or create drama with a series of vases with the same shape but varying heights, each bearing a bloom in the same shade. You'll see grouped arrangements throughout this book; two examples are shown below and on the facing page.

ABOVE: A lavish mixed bouquet, arranged with the aid of floral foam, borrows its lushness and style from Renaissance Dutch and Flemish still lifes like the one shown on the facing page.

BELOW, LEFT: A group of unique vintage bottles, all bearing fritillaries with stems cut to different lengths, makes a harmonious composition in subtle hues.

BELOW: A perfect rose can be an effective arrangement all by itself.

ABOVE: Sunflower varieties grown for cutting
have shorter stems than their giant cousins;
a tall vase helps keep the stems upright
and supports the heavy flower heads.

ABOVE, RIGHT: For a charming and natural
effect, this exuberant mix of summer flowers
and foliage is arranged much as it was
found growing in the garden.

**FROM GARDEN TO VASE.** When you use flowers from your garden, you'll constantly be inspired by what you see—and that means that your arrangements will be fresh and ever-changing. You may come up with entirely unexpected combinations, just because you happen to find the plants growing in the garden at the same time. You'll also learn to look at foliage with a fresh eye when you think of it as a possible addition to your bouquets.

Once you've cut your selections and conditioned them properly (see pages 106–107), you're ready to begin creating your arrangements. As you work, heed the following tips for handling and preparing flowers and containers.

- Always make sure the container is clean before you begin. Scrub it with hot, soapy water and a little bleach (to kill bacteria); then rinse thoroughly.

- Most flowers prefer lukewarm water; cold water is a shock. Some floral designers advise using plain water (and changing it *often* during the life of the arrangement), but others add a pinch of sugar and a drop or two of bleach to the water. Still others use one part lemon-lime soda to two parts water. Many designers frown on commercial floral preservatives for environmental reasons, but you can use them if you prefer.

- When preparing stems for an arrangement, strip off all the leaves that will be below the water line. If they're left on, they can dirty the water and shorten the life of the arrangement.

- Always recut stems under water before you place them in an arrangement. (For more advice on dealing with stems of various kinds, see page 107.)

- Avoid overhandling tender blossoms. If you must lay them down on your work table temporarily, position the flower heads—especially those of easily bruised flowers like irises and some poppies—so they hang over the table edge.

- To determine an appropriate height and width for the arrangement, place the empty container where you plan to display the finished arrangement. If possible, work with the container at the height from which it will be viewed. For example, an arrangement on a foyer table will usually be seen by people who are standing, whereas one on a dining table will be seen by seated guests.

- Just like models and movie stars, every flower has a "good" side. Turn each blossom in your hand to see which side to feature and to determine the natural bend of its stem; then follow the flower's inclinations when placing it in your arrangement.

- As you add flowers to the container, turn it continually to make sure the arrangement is balanced from every side. (The same is true for arrangements you create in your hand; see pages 58–59.)

ABOVE: Terra-cotta pots (without drainage holes, of course) make delightful containers for cut flowers, too.

LEFT: A deep double sink is ideal for conditioning cut flowers in water before arranging.

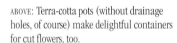

### DESIGNER'S TIP

To freshen cut violets or hydrangeas, submerge them, flowers and all, in cold water for a minute or so. Lift out and give a gentle shake or two. Then wrap violets in damp paper towels; place hydrangeas upright in water and cover the blossom heads with damp paper towels. Leave either kind of flower in a cool, dark place for a couple of hours or overnight before arranging.

# TOOLS, TRICKS, AND TECHNIQUES

*Floral designers use a variety of tools and techniques to create those lovely arrangements. For basic arranging, start by assembling the tools and accessories (the so-called mechanics) described below.*

TOOLS. A few tools will make preparing and arranging your flowers much easier. To avoid damaging tender stems, always have all tools sharp and clean.

Basic flower-arranging tools include hand pruners for cutting woody stems; florist's or other sharp scissors; a stem stripper for removing rose thorns; and a sharp knife for cutting floral foam and some stems. It may also be helpful to keep bottle brushes in several sizes on hand for washing out narrow-necked containers. Other supplies can include bleach; any ingredients you want to use as floral preservatives; and dish soap for washing out containers (see "From garden to vase," page 30).

MECHANICS. If you suit the container's shape and size to the flowers, much of your need for mechanics will be satisfied. For example, a tall, narrow-necked vase may provide adequate support for soft, floppy stems on its own. In some circumstances, however, it may be necessary to bring mechanics into play: when you have a mix of flowers with differing habits and forms; when you're using a vase that fits some flowers but not others; or when you want to create a low table centerpiece or one with fruits, berries, and other nonfloral elements. Some common mechanics are floral foam, frogs, waterproof floral tape, floral adhesive, florist's picks (for securing fruit or berries in arrangements), and sheet or sphagnum moss. Examples of how to use these accessories can be found in descriptions of specific projects in Chapter 3 of this book.

1. Ratchet hand pruners (for cutting twigs and branches)
2. All-purpose hand pruners
3. Knife
4. Stem stripper
5. Bottle brushes
6. Floral foam
7. Sphagnum moss
8. Wire ties
9. Frogs
10. Florist's picks
11. Floral tape
12. Florist's wire

ESSENTIAL TECHNIQUES. When you create arrangements, you'll be using one or more of the techniques outlined here. For more details, see the pages indicated for each technique.

*Building a natural framework of stems.* With this technique, you create a crisscross lattice in the container, using sturdy flower stems and branches. This provides an underwater framework in which to insert flowers with soft or weak stems. (See pages 70–71.)

*Creating an arrangement in your hand.* Floral designers often favor this technique for creating arrangements that aren't too large. It does take some practice, but if you persevere, you'll find it's an excellent way to create a full, rounded bouquet. Begin by holding several flowers; then insert more flowers on all sides, a few at a time, until you have a finished arrangement that's ready to pop into a vase. (See pages 58–59.)

*Doing the twist.* Sometimes called the French twist, this method creates an arrangement in which the bundled stems form a graceful spiral that looks wonderful in a tall clear glass vase. Though often used to create an all-of-a-kind arrangement—especially with bulb flowers like daffodils or callas—the method can also be successfully used with mixed bouquets if all the stems are attractive. (See pages 38–39.)

*Making bundles.* Sometimes it's easiest to make a really dense, full bouquet if you create small bundles of flowers and insert them into your container bundle by bundle. This works very well with an all-of-a-kind arrangement. You can also use it to combine two or three types of flowers; you make one or more bundles of each type and use them to create drifts of color. (See pages 54–55.)

*Using frogs.* Long a staple accessory of flower arrangers, these devices are useful when you need to hold flower stems in place in a shallow bowl, a wide-necked container, or a tiny container like a teacup. The pinholder type (also called a kenzan) is a cushion of sharp pins on which you impale stems; it works especially well with thick or woody stems. "Hairpin" frogs are designed to hold stems between bent wires. Other frogs, whether antique collectibles or newer types, have holes or grid spaces into which you insert stems (see pages 45 and 60). You can also make a clever "natural" frog by using a fresh or dried hydrangea to hold flowers in place. Try it—it really works! (See pages 46–47.)

*Using floral foam.* This easy-to-use material is indispensable for use in a variety of situations, especially if you need more control or want to create a large display quickly. It's most often used for table centerpieces, where the arrangement is typically a low one and the container may be shallow; it's also great in containers that aren't watertight. You can also use floral foam as a base when you want to add elements like fruit and berries that don't have stems. Its main drawbacks? It is not reusable, and it can dry out fairly quickly. (See pages 42–43 and 72–73.)

*Creating a tape grid.* If you want to arrange an assortment of soft-stemmed flowers, this technique is sometimes the only way you can get them to stand up. You create a grid of small openings atop a container using floral tape, then insert your flowers in the openings. The trick here is to be sure you've hidden the tape around the container's edges with plenty of flowers and/or foliage. (See pages 62–63.)

A framework of stems, page 70

Hand-assembled bouquet, page 58

Doing the twist, page 38

Making bundles, page 54

Using frogs, page 46

Using floral foam, page 42

Creating a tape grid, page 62

# FLOWER ARRANGER'S CORNER

*When you bring freshly cut flowers indoors from the garden, you need a convenient spot to condition, cut, and arrange them. The kitchen is the usual place to perform these chores, but when you work there you often have to clear dishes out of the sink or make space on a counter before you can begin. It's better to have a special workplace set aside, and if you're lucky enough to have room for it, it can become one of your favorite little hideaways. You can create space in a mudroom, a laundry room, an extra bathroom, or a basement—anywhere there's a fairly deep sink. Depending on the location, your flower-arranging corner can double as a potting "shed," a place to do ironing and hand laundry, and so forth. Ideally, the space you choose should open directly into the garden, but this certainly isn't essential.*

To make your chosen space practical and workable, you'll need just few basic elements. You'll want a deep sink, counterspace, and storage for flower-arranging tools and materials (see pages 32–33) as well as for vases and other containers. A few shelves and/or cabinets and perhaps a drawer or two will usually accommodate what you need.

Open shelving is great for storing containers, letting you see what you have at a glance—and a collection of favorite vases arranged on a shelf looks decorative, too. Such shelving is easy to add to any space, and lumberyards and home-supply stores carry an assortment of wood and metal shelves you can install yourself (make sure the shelf brackets are firmly mounted into wall studs).

If you have built-in cabinets, that's great! But other options are equally practical and attractive. Consider freestanding furniture such as hutches, Hoosier cabinets, chests of drawers, and bookcases, as well as stacking bins and other storage containers. You can often find wonderful pieces at garage sales, flea markets, and salvage yards. Such sources can also yield double or single sinks. Of course, you can also buy all these items new, either in a home-and-garden store or in one specializing in storage options.

Your flower-arranging corner can be lovely as well as practical. The flowers and the vases used for displaying them are naturally beautiful, and you can also add pretty touches such as floral-motif curtains or a fabric skirt around your sink area. Paint the walls in pastel green, cream, or another soft color, and put a small, washable flower-patterned rug on the floor. Other extras might include botanical prints or a floral still-life poster or painting on the wall, or a bulletin-board display of bouquet ideas clipped from magazines. If there's room, you can even add a chair—cushioned in floral fabric, of course—for relaxing with your favorite gardening magazines.

### FLOWER ARRANGING

# SEASON
# BY
# SEASON

*Every garden season has its glories. From spring's dainty buds and delicate, newborn colors to summer's riot of floral forms and hues, from autumn's rich leaf and flower tones to winter's dramatic contrasts, Nature offers beauty in endless variety.*

*At any time of the year, you can create lovely arrangements of flowers and foliage that will bring your rooms alive with the colors, scents, forms, and textures of the season. In this chapter, you'll learn how to make the most of what every passing month has to offer. For each season, you'll find photographs of gorgeous, imaginative arrangements—plus an explanation of the techniques used to create those compositions. These are followed by listings of favorite flowers for each time of year. Ready to begin? Just turn the page.*

Clustered in an elegant cloisonné bowl, late-summer dahlias light up the room with their sun-drenched colors.

# Daffodil Twist
## CREATING DRAMA WITH SPRING BLOSSOMS AND STEMS

*This lavish arrangement shows off one of spring's sprightliest bulbs in striking fashion. Above the vase's neck, a dome of ruffled golden trumpets glows like sunlight; below, the flowers' fresh green stems, coaxed into a gentle swirl, provide a fascinating linear element. Before arranging the blooms, be sure to condition the stems as described in "Special Stem Treatments," page 107.*

SPRING

TO BEGIN CREATING THE TWIST, take 10 to 12 stems. Holding them about halfway down their length, lay half of them across your palm in one direction; then lay the other half in the other direction to form an X pattern. Continue to add more stems a few at a time, some going one way, others going the other, until the bunch gets too large to hold.

FIRST, DECIDE HOW HIGH ABOVE THE VASE the flowers should be by holding a small bunch of them next to or inside the empty vase. Then fill the vase with water. Now you're ready to cut the flowers to length. Working with a few at a time, use hand pruners to cut all the stems to the length you've chosen.

GENTLY DROP THE BOUQUET INTO THE VASE; the stems should fall into a crisscross pattern. To emphasize the spiral effect, gently lift the whole bunch by the stems, easing the stems around in a circle. Then add more flowers to fill out the arrangement. Carefully insert them one at a time, following the pattern you've already created in the vase.

*Narcissus* 'Tête-a-tête'

**FOR THIS TRULY EXTRAVAGANT LOOK,**
we used four to five dozen daffodils, but
you can achieve lovely (if not quite as lush)
results with a smaller arrangement in a
smaller vase. Whatever the number of flowers,
choose a vase with a neck about 1 inch wider
than the entire bunch of stems will be.

**OLD-FASHIONED FAVORITES**  With their fluffy flower clusters and heady perfume, lilacs evoke delightful memories of Grandmother's garden. To create a can't-miss bouquet almost instantly, combine the cone-shaped lilacs with the rounded flower heads of snowball viburnum. These flowers look loveliest when massed in a natural-looking arrangement—almost as if they were growing in the vase. For the most striking bouquet, use unequal numbers of the two flowers. Gather them with a lavish hand and be sure to include the foliage, which is attractive in its own right. (Strip off leaves that will be below the water line, and slit or pound the ends of the stems as described on page 107.) A galvanized florist's bucket lends just the right air of casual charm, and its tall, narrow shape allows for a big, billowy arrangement.

# SPRING ENCHANTMENTS
## CELEBRATING THE BEAUTIES OF GARDEN, WOODLAND, AND HEDGE

*For almost all of us, certain flowers embody the spirit of spring. Whether blooming in grand profusion on shrubs and trees, scattered low over a grassy field, or rising from a winter-bare garden bed, flowers such as lilacs and early-spring bulbs have a fresh, natural look—and are likewise best used in informal, fairly unstructured arrangements.*

*Leucojum aestivum* 'Gravetye Giant'

Seen before the flowers have been inserted, this lovely container reveals its secrets. The perforated top section is removable; it has six holes into which you can insert flowers, though it's actually designed for holding bulbs (the bulbs rest in the holes, and their roots grow down to reach the water in the container below). For this arrangement, we cut the snowflakes (in the back row) and dainty white alliums taller than the foreground flowers to create a layered look reminiscent of a natural woodland scene. The flowers were inserted in clusters. For a similar arrangement using more readily available containers, you might group several small vases; place the snowflakes and alliums in two or three taller containers, then rank lower ones holding the remaining flowers in front.

**WOODLAND CHARMERS** Though the dainty flowers in this arrangement have become garden favorites, they also grow in the wild, carpeting sun-dappled forest glens. Here, their delicate charm is enhanced by a porcelain container with a hand-painted floral motif that plays up the fresh colors and patterns of flowers and foliage. Blue forget-me-nots and lavender spring star flower front a thicket of snowflakes and alliums, cut taller to form a green-and-white backdrop.

# Springtime Medley
## PAIRING NATURAL PARTNERS—
## BASKETS AND FLOWERS

*For a simple, light-hearted salute to spring, fill a handsome painted basket with a selection of garden flowers in exuberant colors and varied shapes.*

**CUT A PIECE OF PLASTIC** large enough to line the bottom and sides of the basket; be sure you leave enough at the top to fold down. (If the plastic isn't already folded double on the roll, fold it before cutting to make a two-layer piece.) Arrange the plastic along the bottom and sides of the basket, pleating it to fit at the corners; fold the top edges down and tuck them neatly below the basket rim. With a sharp knife, cut the foam blocks in pieces to fill the basket snugly.

**TO ASSEMBLE AN ARRANGEMENT IN A BASKET,** you'll need a roll of two-ply plastic (from a hardware store) for lining the basket, scissors, floral foam, and a sharp knife. The foam usually comes in precut blocks; measure your basket to determine how many blocks will be required to fill it.

**SOAK THE FOAM THOROUGHLY** in clean water; make sure water covers and penetrates each piece. Drain the foam and arrange it in your basket; then add enough water to come a third of the way up the basket's side. Now begin to arrange the flowers, cutting the stems as you go. Mix tall, medium, and short stems. Working stem by stem, first add flowers in a mixture of medium-height and shorter stems, making sure to place enough shorter stems toward the outside to cover the basket's edges. Add the tallest stems last, inserting them where you want to create visual accents. Tuck in greenery to fill in gaps and conceal any edges of the plastic lining that may show. To insert stems into the foam without breaking them, hold each one near the bottom and work in the tip carefully; then gently feed it deeper into the hole.

SPRING

**CLOSELY HARMONIZING COLORS UNITE A DELIGHTFUL MIXED BOUQUET** of orange tulips, salmon pink Oriental poppies, pink ranunculus, magenta anemones, and lavender alstroemerias. Leatherleaf fern and variegated pittosporum contribute a touch of greenery. The basket provides just the right note of informal charm, and its soft green color is a subtle foil for the bright flowers. Floral foam makes it easier to place the flowers artfully, at varying heights and angles.

**ABSTRACT EXPRESSION** Low and narrow channeled, the old-fashioned pansy ring was designed especially to support the flowers' short, weak stems—the better to display their bright faces. Today's version is divided into two semicircles that can be used together or separately, or even placed around the umbrella pole of a patio table. In this stunning contemporary-style tableau, the crystal half-rings sport jewel-toned pansies that pick up the colors of the abstract painting on the wall behind.

**NOT-SO-SHY VIOLETS** Tiny violets make the biggest impact when gathered into a dense cluster. These garden favorites also gain importance beyond their size when arranged in a very small container —here, a prized McCoy planter pot. The soft green of the pot and the vintage Vernon Kiln plate set up as a backdrop enhance the violets' deep purple color. To create a full-looking mini-bouquet like this, use scissors to cut the stems to varying lengths. Then tuck them into the container one by one; place violet leaves around the edges.

# P ETITE T REASURES
## FOCUSING ON THE DAINTY CHARMS OF SPRING'S TINIEST FLOWERS

*Nestled among the tender new grass or showing their sprightly faces in garden borders, violas and other small, short-stemmed flowers offer spring beauty on a miniature scale. Indoors, these flowers invite close-up appreciation when you display them in small bunches, using diminutive containers that match the blossoms' size.*

The secret to creating this arrangement is a tiny but weighty spiked metal frog. Simply set it in the bottom of the cup, holding it in place with a bit of floral adhesive. Add water; then insert the flowers stem by stem, so that they are either wedged between the spikes or, if thicker, are actually impaled on them.

**A CUP OF BLOSSOMS** What could be more delightful than a tiny arrangement in a treasured teacup? Here, a French cup-and-saucer set adorned with a dainty floral design makes the perfect holder for a springtime posy in shades of lavender blue. Star-shaped brodiaeas and fluffy bachelor's buttons are interlaced with catmint, which gives the composition a soft, casual look. The stems are cut quite short, letting the blossoms take center stage. Try this sort of arrangement with other favorite cups—whether delicate china, hand-thrown pottery with a bold-hued glaze, rustic enamel-on-steel, or another style. Choose your flowers accordingly, and keep in mind that some small-scale flowers on tall stems look different and unexpectedly wonderful when cut very short!

# Bold-color Bouquet
## Showcasing Spring's Brightest Colors

*Some spring colors can really sizzle! Vivid magenta parrot tulips and rich royal purple anemones combine with lavender and soft purple hyacinths and grape hyacinths to make a stunning statement in harmonizing colors. The metal container has a quiet elegance that emphasizes the jewel-like brilliance of the flowers.*

PRESS MOSS DOWN INSIDE THE CONTAINER, covering its bottom and sides; let the moss come up higher than the edges of the container. Take your doubled plastic bags, trim off any stiff top edges or ridges, and turn down the tops to make a cuff. Insert the doubled bag into the "nest" created by the moss; tuck the extra moss at the top over the bag edge to hide it. Then half-fill the bag with water.

TO TURN THIS NONWATERTIGHT METAL CONTAINER INTO A VASE, you use doubled quart-size plastic bags to hold the water; these are concealed by a lining of sheet moss, available from florists' suppliers (you could also use sphagnum moss or even moss scraped from paving or other stones in your yard). Finally, a dried or fresh hydrangea head on its stem makes a natural frog (see page 32) that supports the flowers, preventing them from flopping sideways.

CUT THE STEM OF A HYDRANGEA to a height that will place the flower head at or just above the container's top edge; center it in the water-filled bag. Now add your flowers, cutting their stems to varying lengths as you work. Insert the flowers one by one through and around the hydrangea head, making sure the flower stems extend well down into the water. Fill in with enough flowers to conceal the hydrangea almost entirely, especially around the outside edges.

SPRING

**SEVERAL SPECIAL TECHNIQUES** help turn an essentially open metal "basket" into a watertight container for a showstopping arrangement of freshly cut spring bulbs. An almost-hidden hydrangea blossom serves as a natural frog, helping you create a dense, lavish-looking bouquet.

# SPRING

*The favorite spring-flowering plants described here include annuals, perennials, bulbs, and shrubs. Unless otherwise indicated, all need a sunny spot, average to good soil, and regular watering; a few have special climate preferences. Hardiness—the minimum low temperature a plant will tolerate— is noted for all but annuals.*

*Lathyrus odoratus*

## ANNUALS

**ANTIRRHINUM MAJUS. Snapdragon.** Upright, narrow-leafed plant bears dense spikes of distinctive two-lipped flowers in white, cream, lavender, and shades of pink, red, orange, and yellow. Many strains, from 8 inches to 3 feet tall. Performs best in cool to mild weather. In mild-winter areas, it will live over winter.

**CENTAUREA CYANUS. Bachelor's button, cornflower.** Upright, rather wispy plant with very narrow leaves and double, carnationlike flowers to 1½ inches wide; colors include bright blue, white, pink, wine red. Named strains range from 1 to 2½ feet tall.

**CLARKIA.** Two species are good for cutting. Both are upright, narrow-leafed plants. Farewell-to-spring or godetia, *C. amoena*, reaches 2½ feet and has cup-shaped, 2-inch pink or lavender flowers marked in crimson. Mountain garland, *C. unguiculata*, grows 1 to 4 feet high and bears spikes of usually double, 1-inch flowers in purple, pink shades, crimson, orange, cream, and white.

**CONSOLIDA AJACIS (C. AMBIGUA). Larkspur.** Narrow, upright, 1- to 4-foot plant has almost fernlike leaves, long spikes of flowers resembling delphiniums. Colors include blue shades, lilac, pink, rosy red, white, and blue-and-white combinations. Prefers cool weather. Flowers can be dried.

**IBERIS. Annual candytuft.** Hyacinth-flowered candytuft, *I. amara*, grows upright to about 15 inches high; small, fragrant white blossoms come in dense, elongated clusters. Globe candytuft, *I. umbellata*, is the same height but is bushy and rounded. Its flowers come in flattened clusters; colors include white, lilac, pink shades, and crimson.

**LATHYRUS ODORATUS. Sweet pea.** Bears long-stemmed clusters of very fragrant, 1- to 2-inch blossoms with distinctive banner-and-keel shape in many colors and bicolors. Most strains are cool-weather plants. Bush types are available, but the vining kinds are more widely sold and offer a greater color range.

**MATTHIOLA INCANA. Stock.** Intensely fragrant cool-weather annual produces upright spikes of single or double, 1-inch flowers in purple, lavender, pink, crimson, yellow, cream, white. Named strains range from 1 to 3 feet tall. Plant is bushy, with narrow grayish leaves.

**NIGELLA DAMASCENA. Love-in-a-mist.** Upright, 1½- to 2-foot plant bears filmy, threadlike foliage and double, 1½-inch flowers in blue, white, or pink; blossoms resemble bachelor's buttons but are framed by a ruff of threadlike leaves. Balloon-like, horned seedpods can be dried for arrangements.

**PAPAVER. Poppy.** Several kinds bloom in spring, all with satiny, cup-shaped flowers borne singly on slender stems. Among these is Shirley poppy, *P. rhoeas*, a 3-footer with 2- to 3-inch flowers in soft blue, white, pink shades, red, orange, bicolors; it does best in cool weather. Another choice is 4-foot-tall breadbox or opium poppy, *P. somniferum*, with single or double blooms to 5 inches across in red, purple, cool pink, and white.

**VIOLA. Pansy, viola.** Plants are leafy and bushy yet low and sprawling, bearing the familiar flat, five-petaled flowers on individual stems. Pansy (*V. × wittrockiana*) bears 2- to 4-inch flowers in a dazzling array of colors and color combinations; blossoms are often marked with dark, velvety blotches. Viola (*V. cornuta*) is a smaller version of pansy, with a more limited range of colors and patterns. Both are cool-weather plants.

# BULBS AND BULBLIKE PLANTS

ANEMONE CORONARIA. Poppy-flowered anemone. Showy, flat to bowl-shaped flowers to 2½ inches wide come on 6- to 16-inch stems that rise above clumps of fernlike leaves. Flowers may be single, semidouble, or double, in white, pink, red, blue. Do not water during summer. Hardy to 0°F/−18°C. Dig and store over winter in colder regions; dig and store when foliage yellows if you cannot withhold summer water.

CONVALLARIA MAJALIS. Lily-of-the-valley. Broadly oval leaves reach 9 inches long; slim stems peek above the leaves, bearing loose clusters of small, bell-shaped white flowers with a powerfully sweet fragrance. Double-flowered and pink varieties exist. A planting will spread to become a dense colony. Needs winter chill. Hardy to −40°F/−40°C.

*Convallaria majalis*

FREESIA. Fans of foot-tall, narrow leaves send up thin, 1- to 1½-foot stems that bend toward the top, displaying trumpet-shaped, 2-inch flowers that face upward. Original garden favorite is *F. alba*, with creamy white, highly perfumed blossoms; hybrids have flowers in yellow, orange, red, pink, lavender, purple, but not all are as fragrant as the original. Do not water during summer. Hardy to 20°F/−7°C. Dig and store over winter in colder regions; dig and store when foliage yellows if you cannot withhold summer water.

GLADIOLUS. Most widely grown are the Grandiflora hybrids, featuring narrow fans of swordlike leaves and 3- to 6-foot stems bearing two-ranked spikes of trumpet-shaped flowers. Many colors and color combinations, featuring white, cream, yellow, orange, red, pink, purple, lavender. Corms flower roughly 100 days from planting; successive plantings will give you a prolonged display. Hardy to 0°F/−18°C, but most gardeners dig and store over winter in all regions.

IRIS. Flat fans of swordlike leaves send up stems bearing blossoms composed of three upright or arching true petals (standards) and three flaring to drooping, petal-like sepals (falls). Many different types are good for cutting. Flowers come in virtually all colors but true red and green. Bearded irises need moderate to regular watering; many beardless types (Japanese, Louisiana, Siberian) thrive with regular to ample water. Specialty catalogs list multitudinous hybrids. Bearded, Japanese, and Siberian irises are hardy to −35°F/−37°C with protection; Louisianas are hardy to about −15°F/−26°C with protection.

*Freesia*

LEUCOJUM AESTIVUM. Summer snowflake. Narrow, erect, straplike leaves to 1 to 1½ feet; flower stems to 1½ feet bear clusters of pendent, inch-long white bells with green spots around the margins. Blooms in late winter in mildest regions, in spring elsewhere (despite the "summer" name). Hardy to 30°F/−34°C.

NARCISSUS. Daffodil, narcissus. See "Winter" (page 90).

RANUNCULUS ASIATICUS. Persian ranunculus. Double, 3- to 5-inch flowers resembling very full roses (or peonies) come atop slender, 2-foot stems that rise above lush, fernlike foliage. Colors include white, cream, and bright to pastel shades of yellow, orange, red, and pink, plus some bicolor combinations. Quit watering when leaves turn yellow; give no summer water. Hardy to 10°F/−12°C. Dig and store over winter in colder regions; dig and store when foliage yellows if you cannot withhold summer water.

TULIPA. Tulip. Classic bowl- to egg-shaped blossoms appear on slim, upright stems rising from clumps of lancelike to broadly oval leaves. There are many classes of

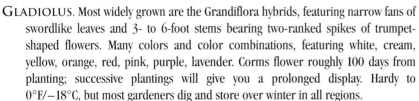

*Zantedeschia aethiopica*

*Heuchera × brizoides*

tulips, based on size, appearance, ancestry. Favorites for cutting are those with stems over a foot tall. Tulips come in all colors but true blue; there are bicolors and decoratively marked types, some with double flowers or fringed petals. All need winter chill and do not perform well in the Deep South and low-elevation Southwest. Even in many cold-winter areas, performance declines after the first year—so gardeners there often buy new bulbs annually. Hardy to −40°F/−40°C.

ZANTEDESCHIA AETHIOPICA. Calla. Elegant, cornucopia-shaped white flowers with a central yellow spike come atop thick green stems 2 to 4 feet tall. Arrow-shaped leaves are 1 to 1½ feet long, on long stalks just shorter than the flower stems. Shorter varieties are available. Takes light shade and will grow in very moist soil as well as in regular garden conditions. Hardy to 0°F/−18°C.

## PERENNIALS

AQUILEGIA. Columbine. Foliage resembles that of maidenhair fern, grows in clumps that send up branched stems 1 to 3 feet high, depending on variety. Blossoms have a central "cup" of petals that rests on a "saucer" of five pointed sepals; spurs often project backward from the flower. Colors include white, blue, purple, pink, red, and yellow, and there are many bicolors. Hybrid strains are easy to find. McKana Giants and Spring Song are potential 3-footers; Dragonfly is at the short end of the height range. Need partial shade except where summers are cool. Hardy to −35°F/−37°C.

DIANTHUS. Carnation, pink. Loved for their spicy clove fragrance as well as their perky, fresh-looking blooms, these flowers range from 1 to 3 inches wide, have pinked to fringed petals, may be single (flat and circular), semidouble, or double. They come singly or in small clusters atop slender, jointed stems (8 to 24 inches long, depending on type) that rise above clumps of narrow, almost grasslike, typically gray-green leaves. Colors include white, pink, red, maroon, yellow, orange; many have contrasting picotee petal margins. Hardy to −35°F/−37°C.

HEUCHERA. Coral bells. Dense clumps of round, scallop-edged leaves send up wire-thin stems with small, nodding, bell-shaped blossoms in airy clusters. *H. sanguinea* bears red, coral pink, or white flowers on 2-foot stems; *H. × brizoides* is a hybrid group of plants to 2½ feet, with blooms in white, pink shades, red. Named varieties are available. Hardy to −30°F/−34°C; not suited to the Deep South.

IBERIS SEMPERVIRENS. Evergreen candytuft. Foot-tall, spreading plants have narrow dark green leaves and 2-inch, nearly flat clusters of small white flowers. Of the many named selections, 'Purity' and 'Snowflake' are good cut-flower varieties. Hardy to −30°F/−34°C; not suited to the Deep South.

LUPINUS. Lupine. Bushy, dense plants have leaves about the size and shape of a hand with outstretched fingers. Stems reach 4 to 5 feet, bearing elegant, tapered spires densely packed with sweet pea–shaped flowers. Modern hybrids come in white, blue, purple, pink, red, orange, yellow, bicolors. Plants need cool summers to grow well. Hardy to −35°F/−37°C.

PAEONIA. Peony. Stems rise from ground level to produce shrubby, 2- to 4-foot plants with many-segmented leaves. Flowers may be single, semidouble, or double (like pompoms) and vary from 2 to 10 inches across; many are fragrant. Colors include white, cream, pink shades, red, maroon. Plants need definite winter chill, do not perform well in the Deep South and much of the low-elevation Southwest. Hardy to −50°F/−46°C.

*Rosa* 'Just Joey'

# SHRUBS

**DEUTZIA.** Deciduous. Plants bear masses of ½- to ¾-inch blossoms in white, pink, red; flowers are trumpetlike, the mouth flaring out to a star shape. Available species and varieties include low, spreading plants 2 to 4 feet high as well as taller, upright ones to 10 feet. Hardy to −20°F/−29°C.

**KOLKWITZIA AMABILIS.** Beautybush. Deciduous. Upright, arching, fountainlike plant can reach 12 feet high. At bloom time, branches are weighed down by ½-inch, bell-shaped, yellow-throated pink flowers. Bristly pinkish brown fruits follow the blossoms, are also good in arrangements. Grows in part shade as well as in sun. Hardy to −20°F/−29°C.

**PHILADELPHUS.** Mock orange. Deciduous. Many choices, from tall, fountainlike plants to low, mounding ones; most are notably fragrant. All bear 1- to 2-inch-wide, four-petaled white blossoms; there are double-flowered varieties. Hardiness varies. Old favorite *P. coronarius* is hardy to −30°F/−34°C, as is *P.* × *virginalis*; *P.* × *lemoinei* is hardy to −10°F/−23°C.

**ROSA.** Rose. Deciduous. See pages 108–109. Hardiness varies, but most modern hybrids can survive to 10°F/−12°C without protection.

**SYRINGA.** Lilac. Deciduous. Best known is common lilac, *S. vulgaris,* a bulky shrub (to 10 to 20 feet high and wide) with dense, conical clusters of small, intensely fragrant blossoms in white, blue, lavender, purple, wine red, pink. Many named varieties are sold. Plants need definite winter chill, though 'Lavender Lady' performs with minimal cold. Hardy to −40°F/−40°C.

*Viburnum opulus* 'Roseum'

**VIBURNUM.** Snowball. Deciduous. Several viburnums bear dense, round "snowballs" of white flowers. Fragrant snowball, *V.* × *carlcephalum* (hardy to −10°F/−23°C), grows 10 feet high and wide and bears 5-inch, sweet-scented blossom clusters. Common snowball, *V. opulus* 'Roseum' (to −40°F/−40°C), is an arching plant to 15 feet tall; flower clusters are 2½ inches wide. Japanese snowball, *V. plicatum* (*V. tomentosum* 'Sterile'; to −10°F/−23°C), is a horizontally branching plant to 15 feet high, bearing 3-inch flower clusters. (For viburnums grown for their fruit, see page 111.)

**WEIGELA.** Deciduous. Flowers resembling small white, pink, or red foxgloves cover plants that vary from upright and arching to mounding and spreading. Named varieties are available. Needs some winter chill. Hardy to −20°F/−29°C.

# A Garden on Your Table

*Dining alfresco is one life's great pleasures. And what could be a more natural table decoration for an outdoor meal than flowers and greenery snipped from your own borders and beds? Such arrangements let you enjoy your garden twice over as you dine, admiring its colorful beauty both close up, in a cut-flower bouquet, and from a distance.*

Whether you use them indoors or out, table arrangements offer lots of room for creativity. Along with a variety of flowers, they may include fruit, vegetables, and greenery. Candles contained in glass hurricane lamp chimneys or other holders are another popular addition—and in fact, the soft glow of candlelight is one of the most appealing features of an evening meal outside.

CENTERPIECES The key to creating successful table arrangements, especially those to be displayed in an outdoor setting, is to keep them simple and fairly unstructured, so they reflect the relaxed spirit of the garden. Of course, their size and style will still vary with the occasion. One factor to consider is the way the meal is served—is it a sit-down affair or a buffet? In the former case, the main arrangement should be fairly low, so diners can easily see and talk to each other. For a casual family meal, you might set out an uncomplicated clutch of daisies, sweet peas, or other favorites, loosely

arranged in a bright, plump ceramic vase or a colored glass bottle. If you're gathered around an umbrella table, try using a ring-shaped container with separate halves that can encircle the umbrella pole, and fill it with an assortment of favorite flowers such as cosmos, zinnias, and dahlias. Or put a few small, low vases or bottles, each holding one or two blooms, here and there on the tabletop.

If you're serving buffet style, you can create a taller, fuller arrangement that functions as a lavish backdrop for the dishes and the food itself—just as you would for an indoor meal. One appealing example is shown above: a fresh-looking mix of purple alliums, lavender irises, rosy peonies, and yellow lupine, trimmed with a lacy green "skirt" of maidenhair fern. If you've set up both a big buffet table and smaller individual tables, you might adorn the buffet with a large arrangement, then dress up the small tables with smaller, coordinating bouquets featuring just one or two of the flowers used in the main arrangement. You can also use such smaller arrangements in a more casual set-up, where guests aren't seated at tables but simply on benches, chairs, and so forth—just scatter the bouquets on a wide deck railing or a patio side table.

Though dining table centerpieces are generally assembled in low bowls, pans, or perhaps baskets, the taller buffet arrangements allow you more latitude. Use large vases, pitchers, or other showy containers. Or stack two or three pedestal cake plates, then decorate each tier with clustered small vases or glasses of flowers or with lush assortments of fruit and blossoms.

MULTIPLE ARRANGEMENTS A very simple way to dress up tables of any size—buffet or otherwise—is to use a series of small arrangements. Opt for a variety of containers and flower types; or choose multiple matching containers holding identical flowers, such as the charming glass cubes brimming with tulips and Boston ivy shown below. Scatter these little beauties around the table or set one at each place. You might even grace each place setting with a floral take-home party favor: a tiny arrangement in a miniature vase, bottle, or other container, or perhaps a nosegay of fresh flowers tied together with raffia or ribbon (not long lasting, but lots of fun!).

SMALL TOUCHES Finally, you can add that extra touch of elegance with lovely small details, such as napkins "trimmed" with fresh blossoms. Try specially designed napkin rings such as the sweet pea–filled glass loops pictured above; or simply tie a rolled napkin with a ribbon or raffia, then tuck in a flower or two.

Another fresh and flowery idea is to wrap individual place settings of silverware or (as shown below) servings of sandwiches in parchment paper, tie them with ribbon or twine, and slip a blossom or two beneath the tie.

# ZINNIAS BY THE BUNDLE
## CREATING A LAVISH ALL-OF-A-KIND BOUQUET

*With their carnival-bright colors and round, cheery faces, these summertime favorites make a delightful all-of-a-kind bouquet. Gathering the stems into a number of small bundles before assembling them in a container assures a dense, fully packed display of the sort Europeans call a pavé arrangement.*

CUT THE STEMS TO SLIGHTLY DIFFERENT LENGTHS, so that the flowers will form a smoothly graduated dome when arranged in the bowl. Strip off all leaves with your fingers. Divide the flowers into groups of four to six stems of varying lengths (you can see, for example, that the yellow zinnia is slightly taller). Each group will form a separate bundle.

A WIDE, SHALLOW BOWL makes a good container for creating a colorful floral dome. This good-sized bowl required four to five dozen stems; a smaller one would fill up with fewer blossoms. You'll need pruners to cut the zinnias' thick stems cleanly. For securing the bundles of blooms, have wire ties, florist's wire, or rubber bands on hand.

GENTLY SECURE EACH BUNDLE WITH A WIRE TIE just below the flower heads; then place the bundles in the bowl one by one, beginning around the edges and building from there to form a dome shape.

**ZINNIAS ARE NATURAL DAZZLERS.** Make the most of
their brilliance by planting them in drifts by color, then picking
an armload in closely related hues to make a stunning bouquet.
Bundling is the secret to the lavish look.

**ROSES BY THE DOZEN** If you have a particularly vigorous rose or grow many plants of the same color and type, you can create a lavish all-of-a-kind bouquet like this one. More than two dozen 'Pat Austin' roses in a delicious shade of peach make the ultimate romantic offering. For a natural and ever-changing look, we combined blooms in various stages of development; a few geranium leaves were added to soften the transition between flowers and vase. The secret to the arrangement's success is a hidden grid of floral tape that holds stems in position (see "Rainbow Bouquet," pages 62–63).

**OPPOSITES ATTRACT** This study in contrasts makes for a different and dramatic bouquet. Silky red hybrid tea roses—the traditional flowers of romance—are paired with spiky-looking pink dahlias. Both kinds of flowers have big, showy faces, and they balance one another perfectly when arranged in equal numbers. A branch of curly willow coiled in the bottom of the globe-shaped vase acts as a natural frog to hold the stems in place.

# ROMANCING THE ROSE
## ENHANCING YOUR ROOMS WITH THE ROMANCE OF ROSE BOUQUETS

*As all devoted rose fanciers know, you can never have enough roses! Indoors or out, the "queen of flowers" lends beauty and romance to any setting. Roses are versatile, too: depending on whether they're used as the stars of the show or partnered with other flowers, they can have very different looks, as these photos so beautifully demonstrate. For tips on growing roses for cutting, see pages 108–109.*

**SWEETHEART BOUQUET** Roses and hydrangeas might have been made just for each other, as witness this charming hearts-and-flowers bouquet. The fluffy white hydrangeas form a bed of clouds for sweet pink roses. The roses' stems are cut fairly short, then inserted one by one among the hydrangea heads, which hold them in place. (For more on using hydrangeas as natural frogs, see pages 46–47.)

# OLD-FASHIONED POSY
## REVIVING A TRADITION WITH COTTAGE-GARDEN BLOOMS

*The charming custom of presenting a loved one with a small, beribboned bunch of flowers—variously called a posy or a tussie-mussie—lives on in this contemporary bouquet, displayed in a pretty vase. You create the arrangement right in your hand.*

GATHER FLOWERS in the cool of the morning, if possible. The 'Iceberg' roses shown here are floribundas that bear clustered blooms, perfect for filling out flower arrangements. Clusters of sweet peas also contribute lushness. When using the technique shown on these pages, you'll have the most success working with a small number of flowers—only as many stems as will fit comfortably in your hand.

KEEP ADDING BUNCHES OF FLOWERS, alternating sides to achieve a pleasing balance of forms and colors. When the bouquet is complete, secure the stems with a rubber band. Place your bouquet in the vase for a moment to see how high the flowers should rise above the vase. Be sure the rubber band will be level with the top of the vase, so that the ribbon tie (see below) will show. Using sharp pruners, clip the stems level across the bottom.

SEPARATE FLOWERS into piles by variety; lay each pile flat on a table. Begin by placing a cluster of roses in your hand, holding them a few inches below the flower heads. Now start filling in the arrangement, working with one type of flower at a time. Here, cosmos have been added; bachelor's buttons will go in next.

TIE A RIBBON AROUND THE STEMS to hide the rubber band, pop your posy into the water-filled vase, and voila! You've created a charming and spontaneous-looking arrangement.

THIS MIXED BOUQUET features a selection of cottage-garden favorites you can enjoy for their fragrance as well as for their charming forms and colors. Bright white 'Iceberg' roses and a sprinkling of blue bachelor's buttons add punch to pink cosmos and sweet peas.

**HIGH STYLE** Elegant and dramatic, gladioli are a natural choice for spectacular cut flowers. Their tall spikes, set with rows of ruffled blooms in a rich variety of colors, make stunning accents for mixed arrangements—and they're even more striking in an all-of-a-kind bouquet. Arranged in a relatively flat fan shape, the grand flowers are a good choice for a narrow space like a side table, where a more rounded arrangement might bump into the wall behind.

THE STIFFNESS OF THEIR STEMS makes glads a cinch to arrange; just be sure to choose a vase tall enough to balance their height. Using a hairpin frog anchored with floral adhesive will help you achieve the fan shape pictured above and provide support for the tall stems. Simply ease the stems, one by one, into place between the wire loops.

*Gladiolus,* Grandiflora hybrid

**BACK-FENCE CHARMERS**  With their fresh, clean colors and delightful perfume, sweet peas have long been garden favorites. These old-fashioned flowers look charming in almost any container, but the soft gleam of silver sets off their lovely hues especially well. When you use a relatively tall container like the vintage coffeepot shown here, cut the sweet peas' stems as long as possible and let the blossoms spread in a natural, unstudied manner.

# CLASSICS REVISITED
## ARRANGING CLASSIC FLOWERS
## FROM GARDENS PAST

*Some flowers never fall from favor. Whether associated with Victorian high style or grand-mother's garden, whether enjoyed as dramatic displays or intimate delights, they are loved by gardeners and flower arrangers alike for their timeless beauty and charm.*

**CAN'T-MISS FAVORITES**  Long-time favorites among flowering shrubs, hydrangeas have an unrivaled, full-blown charm. Whether they're the lace-cap or mophead type, the huge, fluffy flowers are can't-miss selections for bouquets. Just a modest bunch fills a bowl generously and almost arranges itself: the full flower heads support each other. Whether you select blooms in one color or mix two or more hues (as shown here), the effect is always spectacular. Our bouquet is displayed in a moss-lined metal basket; to learn how to prepare such a container, see pages 46–47. For a special hydrangea conditioning tip, see page 31.

# RAINBOW BOUQUET
## GATHERING A RICH ARRAY OF SUMMER BLOOMS

*Creating a spectacular mixed bouquet like this one is something of a challenge: starting with flowers in all kinds of forms and colors, you must somehow create an harmonious whole. To make the job easier turn to a flower arranger's secret—a tape grid that lets flowers with differing stem heights and habits work successfully together, producing an arrangement with a soft, unstructured look.*

WHEN YOU'VE SPANNED THE BOWL'S MOUTH completely in one direction, add strips going in the other direction, forming a grid. The openings should be about ¼ inch square; if they're too large, the flower stems will simply flop.

TO CREATE THIS ARRANGEMENT IN A WIDE BOWL, you'll need waterproof floral tape (either green, as shown here, or clear) to make a grid across the top of the bowl. Cut strips one at a time, making each long enough to extend past the bowl's lip by about ½ inch on either side. Fasten them across the bowl, parallel and about ¼ inch apart.

INSERT FLOWER STEMS IN THE GRID SPACES one at a time, placing some of the taller stems in the center and distributing shorter ones around the periphery. As the arrangement begins to take shape, you'll find that the first stems you placed will help support those added later. Keep on tucking in flowers, rotating the bowl so the arrangement is full and balanced on all sides. To hide the tape, be sure to fill in with plenty of greenery and trailing stems around the edge of the bowl.

THE SUMMER GARDEN'S RICHES are gathered
with a generous hand for a look that's at once exuberant
and controlled. The exuberance is in the spirited selection;
the control is in the hidden mechanics that let you combine
the blossoms so beautifully. Flowers as diverse as cherry red
dahlias, deep salmon lilies (some still in bud), green bells-
of-Ireland, lavender pincushion flower, purple delphiniums,
and purple-and-white lisianthus are punctuated with a
few small sunflowers and trimmed with a yellow-green
flounce of lady's-mantle.

**SUN-DRENCHED COLOR**  This eye-popping bouquet, also featured on our cover, contains an exuberant mix of red dahlias, 'teddy bear' sunflowers, purple larkspur, and lavender catmint. The blossoms blaze from a rustic half-glazed earthenware jug, calling to mind a European country garden where beds overflow with color behind ancient, sun-baked walls. This arrangement was created using the hand-held method (see pages 58–59).

# SUMMER DAZZLERS
## SHOWCASING SUMMER'S BRILLIANCE

*There's nothing shy and retiring about the bright, cheerful colors of the summer garden! Show off the season's dazzling flowers indoors, too, in large, splashy mixed bouquets or in smaller bunches with old-fashioned appeal.*

**BRIGHT AND SIMPLE**

Sometimes simple is best, as this little vase of crayon-bright nasturtiums demonstrates. The curvy green stems are decoratively crisscrossed in a glass container; the ruffled blossoms cluster above. Besides being pretty, nasturtiums are edible. Try sprinkling washed, pesticide-free leaves and flowers in a green salad; they'll add a pleasantly peppery flavor and a touch of cheery color.

**A BIT OF NOSTALGIA**

Conjuring up visions of lawn chairs and ice-cold lemonade, black-eyed Susans embody the essence of an old-fashioned summer. Their daisylike blooms make lovely, natural-looking bouquets: just gather them into a full, rounded bunch and pop them into an unpretentious container like this white ceramic pitcher. Cut the flowers for indoor display as often as you want— cutting encourages rebloom late in the season.

# SUMMER

*Annuals and perennials dominate the summer cut-flower scene. The plants described here put on their main show only in summer; for those that continue blooming well into fall, see "Summer and Autumn" (page 79). All need a sunny spot, average to good soil, and regular watering unless otherwise noted; a few have special climate preferences. Hardiness—the minimum low temperature a plant will tolerate—is noted for all but annuals.*

*Cleome hassleriana*

## ANNUALS

**AGERATUM HOUSTONIANUM.** Floss flower. Dense clusters of tiny blue, pink, or white flowers look like powder puffs, decorating plants clothed in soft, hairy, heart-shaped leaves. Taller types are best for cutting. Blue-blossomed 'Blue Horizon' grows to 2½ feet; 'Capri' and 'Southern Cross' are 1-footers with white-centered blue flowers. Needs partial shade in all but cool-summer climates.

**ALCEA ROSEA.** Hollyhock. Clumps of large, nearly round leaves send up tall spikes of saucer-shaped, 3- to 6-inch-wide flowers in white, cream, yellow, red, pink, maroon, purple, even nearly black; some have contrasting centers. Most grow about 6 feet tall. Two double-flowered strains are Chater's Double (perennial in much of the West) and Summer Carnival.

**CLEOME HASSLERIANA (C. SPINOSA).** Spider flower. Shrubby, branching plant grows 4 to 6 feet high and nearly as wide, producing large, open clusters of pink or white flowers with protruding stamens that give the blooms a spidery look. Seed capsules can be dried for arrangements. Stems of some are thorny. Named selections have flowers in rosy red, lavender, purple, and white.

**EUSTOMA GRANDIFLORUM.** Lisianthus. Elegant, satiny, bell-shaped, 2- to 3-inch flowers come on stems that reach 3 feet high in the tallest strains. Colors include cream, white, blue, purple, pink, rosy red. Plant in sun or light shade; best growth comes where summer nights are warm.

**MOLUCCELLA LAEVIS.** Bells-of-Ireland. Upright plants to 3 feet high carry elongated spikes of cup-shaped, 1-inch flowers—but what look like petals are in fact apple green calyxes that form a cup around the tiny white true blossoms. Flowers can be used fresh or dried. Grows best in dry-summer regions.

**NICOTIANA ALATA.** Flowering tobacco. Hybrids of this species, often cataloged as *N. × sanderae,* encompass a range of heights and colors. Plants are erect and branching, with slightly sticky leaves and clusters of trumpetlike flowers that flare open to five-lobed stars; many are fragrant. Tallest types grow to 3 feet or a bit higher; these include Daylight Sensation strain, with blooms in white, lavender, purple, and pink, and Heavenscent, bearing strongly perfumed flowers in white, pink, red, and purple. Nicki strain reaches 1½ feet high, has a wider color range that includes red and green. Grow in sun or partial shade.

**RUDBECKIA HIRTA.** Gloriosa daisy, black-eyed Susan. Clumps of lance-shaped, sandpapery leaves send up thin, 3- to 4-foot stems topped with dark-centered daisies in warm colors. Blooms reach 3 to 9 inches across, depending on strain. Best for cutting are taller strains like Gloriosa Daisy and double-flowered Gloriosa Double Daisy, and named varieties such as 'Indian Summer' and green-centered 'Irish Eyes' ('Green Eyes').

## PERENNIALS

**ACHILLEA.** Yarrow. Many species and varieties, all of which feature tiny flowers in showy, flat-topped clusters that are attractive fresh or dried. Fernleaf yarrow, *A. filipendulina,* reaches 3 to 5 feet; the selection 'Gold Plate' has 6-inch clusters of bright yellow flowers. A popular hybrid is dark yellow 'Coronation Gold', with 3-inch flower heads on 3-foot stems. Bright yellow *A. × taygetea* has 2-inch clusters on 1½-foot stems; *A.* 'Moonshine' has 2½-inch clusters of primrose yellow flowers. Hardy to −40°F/−40°C.

ALCHEMILLA MOLLIS. Lady's-mantle. Nearly circular, ruffle-edged gray-green leaves to 6 inches across form foliage mounds to 2½ feet high and wide. Multi-branched flowering stems present an airy froth of tiny greenish yellow blossoms. Needs partial shade in all but cool-summer regions. Hardy to −35°F/−37°C.

ALSTROEMERIA. Peruvian lily. Plants are famous for exotic, azalealike flowers in white, cream, yellow, orange, red, pink, and lilac, often with contrasting markings. The leafy flowering stems rise directly from the ground. Deciduous types (such as the Ligtu hybrids) produce 2- to 5-foot flowering stems as plants die down in late spring. Evergreen types (Cordu, Inca, Meyer, and Premier series, for example), also 2 to 5 feet high, bloom over a longer season. Plants need cool soil. Give them afternoon shade where summers are hot. Hardy to 0°F/−18°C.

ASCLEPIAS TUBEROSA. Butterfly weed. Clumps of upright stems to 3 feet high bear broad, flat-topped clusters of small, star-shaped orange blossoms; forms with yellow, red, and pink flowers are sold. Needs well-drained soil but requires only moderate watering. Hardy to −35°F/−37°C.

*Asclepias tuberosa*

ASTILBE. False spiraea. Tiny flowers are grouped together in branching, conical clusters displayed above clumps of elegant, finely divided foliage. Named hybrids belonging to *A. × arendsii* include plants with white, lavender, pink, and red flowers on stems from 1½ to 4 feet high. Plants need moist, rich soil, some winter chill. Give partial shade in all but cool-summer regions. Not for areas where summers are hot and dry, nor for the Deep South. Hardy to −30°F/−34°C.

BAPTISIA AUSTRALIS. Blue false indigo. Dense, shrubby plant reaches 4 feet high and wide. Leaves are cloverlike; blue-violet, sweet pea–shaped flowers are carried in spikes. Inflated-looking seedpods can be dried for arrangements. Plants take poor to average soil, need only moderate watering. Hardy to −35°F/−37°C.

CAMPANULA. Bellflower. Great variety of plants with bell-shaped to starlike flowers. Taller, upright kinds are best for cutting. *C. lactiflora* reaches 3½ to 5 feet tall, its leafy stems topped in clusters of open, 1-inch bells in white, light blue, or pink. Peach-leafed bluebell, *C. persicifolia,* has 2- to 3-foot stems topped with cup-shaped white, blue, or pink flowers; 'Telham Beauty' has 3-inch blue blossoms. Double-flowered varieties are available. Need partial shade in all but cool-summer regions. Hardy to −30°F/−34°C.

CENTRANTHUS RUBER. Jupiter's beard. Elongated, fluffy clusters of tiny white, dusty pink, or carmine red flowers come at the ends of 3-foot stems on a bushy plant with gray-green foliage. This is a tough plant that grows in sun or partial shade, needs only moderate watering. Hardy to −20°F/−29°C.

CHRYSANTHEMUM MAXIMUM. Shasta daisy. Classic white daisy comes in named varieties offering single and double flowers that range from 3 to 6 inches across; stems vary from 1½ to 4 feet tall and rise from spreading clumps of linear, tooth-edged leaves. Give partial shade in hot-summer regions. Hardy to −35°F/−37°C.

COREOPSIS. Bright yellow daisies come at ends of needle-thin stems above low clumps of narrow leaves. The following two species, both with 1- to 2-foot stems, are good for cutting. *C. grandiflora* bears blooms to 3 inches across; 'Sunburst', 'Sunray', and 'Early Sunrise' have semidouble flowers. Flowers of *C. lanceolata* reach 2 inches across. Both are hardy to at least −30°F/−34°C.

*Coreopsis grandiflora*
'Early Sunrise'

*Dahlia*

*Penstemon × gloxinioides*
'Garnet'

DAHLIA. Shrubby, lushly foliaged plants offer a stunning array of flower colors (all but true blue) and sizes (2 to 12 inches); flower form varies widely as well, though all are daisy-type blossoms (fully double, in most kinds). Specialists offer the widest selection, but nurseries carry a representative sample. Dahlias need rich soil, light shade in hottest climates; tall types require staking. Plants are hardy to 20°F/−7°C, but growers in all climates usually dig the tuberous roots in fall, store them over winter, and replant in spring.

DELPHINIUM. The epitome of elegance! Clumps of fan-shaped, deeply cut leaves send up blossom spires (5 to 8 feet high, in the tallest strains) packed with multi-petaled, 1½- to 2½-inch flowers in blue shades, white, purple, pink, rosy magenta. Pacific and Centurion strains are the tallest; named selections are available. Performance is best where summers are cool to warm (but not hot) and air is moist. Plants need rich soil and require partial shade except where summers are cool. Hardy to −35°F/−37°C.

ECHINACEA PURPUREA. Purple coneflower. Clumps of rough-textured, elongated leaves send up 2½- to 4-foot stems bearing rosy purple, 4-inch daisies with dark, beehivelike centers. In wild forms, petals bend downward from the central cone, but some selections have outward-flaring petals. Named varieties also offer other colors—white, pink, rosy red. Give moderate to regular water. Hardy to −35°F/−37°C.

GERBERA JAMESONII. Transvaal daisy. Elegant single to double daisies to 5 inches across, in clear, bright shades of yellow, orange, red, coral, pink, cream. Blossoms appear individually on 1½-foot stems that rise above clumps of tongue-shaped, lobed leaves. In mild-winter regions, blooms again in late fall. Hardy to 15°F/−9°C; grow as annual in colder regions.

GYPSOPHILA PANICULATA. Baby's breath. The classic "filler" plant for bouquets, this is an intricately branched, almost tumbleweed-like plant spangled with ¼-inch white or pink flowers. Old favorite 'Bristol Fairy' bears double white flowers, grows 4 feet high and wide; 'Perfecta' is similar but has larger (½-inch) flowers. Plants prefer nonacid soil and moderate water, may need staking to keep from sprawling. Hardy to −35°F/−37°C.

LIATRIS SPICATA. Gayfeather. Clumps of narrow, grasslike leaves send up leafy, 4-foot stems topped by foxtail-like spikes of small flowers with prominent stamens. Flowers first open at the top of the spike; then bloom progresses downward. 'Kobold' is a popular 2- to 2½-foot variety with rosy lilac flowers; 'Floristan White' grows to 3 feet. Hardy to −35°F/−37°C.

MONARDA. Bee balm. Bushy, leafy clumps produce upright stems crowned with shaggy-looking clusters of tubular, two-lipped flowers. Height ranges from 2 to 4 feet, depending on variety; colors include white, pink, red, violet. Leaves have a minty aroma. Plants need plenty of water, light shade in hottest regions; they perform best with some winter chill. Hardy to −35°F/−37°C.

PENSTEMON. Many types native to western states are offered by specialty growers; most thrive with little water. For regular garden conditions, however, the following two penstemons shine. Both have upright spikes of flowers resembling foxgloves. *P. digitalis* grows 3 to 5 feet high and has white to pink flowers; its 3-foot variety 'Husker Red' has maroon leaves, blush white flowers. Plants are hardy to −30°F/−34°C. Border penstemon, *P. × gloxinioides,* makes bushy, 2- to 4-foot clumps. Named varieties are available with flowers in white, pink, red, violet, lavender; colored blooms often have white throats. Plants are hardy to 10°F/−12°C and are not perennial outside the western U. S.

PHLOX. Upright clumps of leafy, 3- to 5-foot stems are topped by dome-shaped clusters of flat-faced, five-segmented flowers in white, pink shades, soft orange, red, magenta, and lavender, often with a contrasting central eye. Thick-leaf phlox, *P. maculata,* flowers in early summer; leaves resist mildew. Border phlox, *P. paniculata,* blooms in midsummer and is prone to mildew as summer progresses. Both prefer cool to mild summer temperatures; give them afternoon shade where summers are hot. Both are hardy to −35°F/−37°C.

PLATYCODON GRANDIFLORUS. Balloon flower. Upright, leafy stems rise to 3 feet. At stem tips, buds resembling violet-blue balloons on slender stalks open to five-petaled, starlike, 2-inch flowers. White, pink, and double-flowered varieties are available. Give plants light shade where summers are hot. Hardy to −35°F/−37°C.

SCABIOSA. Pincushion flower. Rising above low foliage clumps, slender stems support spherical, 2- to 3-inch flower heads with numerous protruding stamens that look something like pins in a pincushion. *S. caucasica,* to 2½ feet, has green leaves and flowers in blue, lavender, or white; it needs partial shade in hot-summer regions and is hardy to −35°F/−37°C. Similar *S. columbaria* has gray-green leaves and bears 2- to 3-inch lavender-blue, pink, or white flower heads on 2-foot stems. It is hardy to −20°F/−29°C.

VERONICA SPICATA. Speedwell. Dense foliage mounds send up very slender, 2-foot spikes densely set with small flowers with conspicuous stamens. Bright blue is the standard color; variations are white 'Icicle' and rosy red 'Rotfuchs' ('Red Fox'), both a little under 2 feet high. Hardy to −35°F/−37°C.

*Scabiosa columbaria*
'Pink Mist'

# SHRUBS

BUDDLEJA DAVIDII. Butterfly bush. Deciduous. Fountainlike, narrow-leafed shrubs reach as high as 12 feet, bear a profusion of tapered, arching flower spikes to 1 foot long. Small, fragrant blooms are lilac with an orange eye in the species, but named varieties offer blooms in white, deep blue, violet, reddish purple. 'Harlequin' has purple flowers and cream-variegated leaves. *B. d. nanhoensis* is a smaller form, to 5 feet high and wide. Hardy to −20°F/−29°C.

HYDRANGEA MACROPHYLLA. Bigleaf hydrangea. Deciduous. This is the familiar "mophead" hydrangea, bearing volleyball-size flower heads on bulky, large-leafed shrubs 4 to 8 feet high and wide. The showiest kinds have heads of 1- to 2-inch flowers in white, pink, rosy red, lavender, or blue. French hybrids (the standard florist's fare) are smaller plants, to about 3 feet tall. Flower color can be altered by soil: acid soils produce blue flowers, alkaline ones produce pink to nearly red blooms. Plants need partial shade in all but cool-summer regions. Hardy to −10°F/−23°C.

ROSA. Rose. Deciduous. See pages 108–109. Hardiness varies, but most modern hybrids can survive to 10°F/−12°C without protection.

*Buddleja davidii*

# STATELY STEMS
## BUILDING A BETTER BOUQUET

*Beautiful in their own right, branches of autumn leaves and fruits fill a double role in harvest-season bouquets. Besides combining perfectly with fall blossoms, they serve as natural mechanics, supporting the flowers you use and coaxing the composition into a pleasing shape. Of course, you can use branches or sturdy-stemmed flowers in this way at any time of year—but in autumn, when so many trees and bushes sport vivid foliage or clusters of bright berries, your choices are especially wide and varied.*

SELECT A FEW OF THE STRONGEST, thickest branches and crisscross them in the vase to make a framework for subsequent additions. Now begin to cut your flower stems to size; to decide on the proper height, hold them next to the branch-filled vase before you cut. For a smoothly graduated look, have some flower heads fanning out about midway between the vase's neck and the tops of the branches, others resting just above the neck.

HOLD THE BRANCHES UPRIGHT against the vase first to determine their desired height; you'll want them to rise high enough to define the arrangment's basic outline. With strong ratchet pruners, trim the branch ends as needed, making clean, angled cuts. Then use your pruners to slit the stems an inch or two up from the base; this will help them absorb water efficiently.

FILL IN THE ARRANGEMENT by inserting stems one by one, weaving them into the spaces between the other branches and stems. You'll find that they tend to hold each other upright. Note that not all the stems need reach the bottom of the vase; the framework you've created will allow you to position some higher in the arrangement.

TWO KINDS OF BRANCHES—some bearing colorful maple leaves, others laden with small green persimmons—complement and support a gathering of cheery sunflowers and coreopsis in sunshine colors. A tall, square-sided glass vase is the perfect container choice, permitting a clear view of the handsome stems and giving the arrangement its stately height.

**GRACE NOTES** Arching branches of beautyberry, thickly set with clusters of shiny rose-purple fruit, rise gracefully from puffs of fall-blooming hydrangeas. The container's rounded form and subtle color echo the hydrangeas' shape and hue—and set off the brilliance of the berries. The fluffy hydrangea heads help hold the tall beautyberry stems in place.

**AUTUMN BASKET** Celebrating the many shades of fall, this festive basket sports red chrysanthemums, shiny ornamental peppers, orange-tinted love-in-a-puff, and foliage in shades of plum, green, and rust—from heavenly bamboo, protea and pin oak. The plastic-lined basket hides a water-soaked block of florist's foam; for details, see pages 42–43.

# LATE BLOOMERS
## SHOWCASING AUTUMN'S COLORFUL FLOWERS

*The autumn cutting garden is a treasure trove of rich colors— some glowing with the depth and intensity of gemstones, others soft and almost faded, like vintage fabric. Used in arrangements, late-season blooms such as asters, zinnias, gloriosa daisies, some sunflowers, and hydrangeas blend well with berries and foliage, letting you create bouquets with a unique seasonal character.*

AUTUM N

**ACCENT ON COLOR** This arrangement plays with the color purple, enhancing it with other, warmer colors from the fall garden. The intense violet tones come from clusters of delicate statice and long spikes of Mexican bush sage; accent colors are provided by orange-red cotoneaster berries, orange lantana, and shaggy lion's tail. For a final shot of color, we added bright yellow gloriosa daisies. Pin oak leaves fill out the composition. Arranged asymmetrically, the oak leaves and larger flowers fill in the base; the wispier blossom spikes add interest at the top and trail along the edges.

*Rudbeckia hirta* 'Marmalade'

THOROUGHLY SOAK a large block of floral foam in water. Then use a sharp knife to cut it into one large and one small piece to fit a 10-inch-diameter plastic pot saucer. Slice off the corners as shown, then secure the foam to the saucer with florist's tape. If you have a lazy Susan, place the foam-filled saucer on it so you can rotate it as you work. Or just turn the arrangement occasionally or walk around it, making sure it looks full and balanced on all sides. Push the blunt end of a florist's pick partially into each fruit, leaving the pointed end free to insert into the foam. Also use florist's picks to wire together individual leaves or small leaf clusters.

# HARVEST BOUNTY
## CREATING A FALL CENTERPIECE

*Flowering cabbage, autumn foliage and fruits, and a few blossoms go into a classic table centerpiece that enhances any fall gathering, from casual company supper to grand Thanksgiving feast. Use the materials we show here; or put together any pleasing combination of similar leaves, fruits, and flowers.*

INSERT LONG STRANDS of foliage, grasses, and sprigs of berries at the ends of the large foam piece; let them fan out. Stick additional sprigs horizontally into the sides of the foam, low enough to let them rest on the saucer rim. The material should radiate from the center, like the spokes of a wheel.

PLACE LARGE FOCAL PIECES, such as pomegranates and the flowering cabbage, near the center of the arrangement; place smaller and more delicate materials at the ends. Use bold leaves to accentuate the fruits and berries; add flowers if you want still more color. Once you've placed the finished centerpiece on your table, add a little water to the saucer (plan to replenish it if you want the centerpiece to last for a while).

**THIS FESTIVE ASSEMBLAGE** features a spectacular cream-and-green flowering cabbage surrounded by a rich assortment of autumn's bounty: apples, pomegranates, colorful leaves, red heavenly bamboo berries, small olive branches laden with green fruit, green winter wheat, and dill. Add blossoms too, if you like—we chose vivid coral freesias, but fall flowers from the garden would look just as lovely. If you don't grow flowering cabbage or kale, buy small plants from a nursery, then remove the soil and submerge the plants briefly in water before using them.

*Liquidambar styraciflua*
'Palo Alto'

**QUIET ELEGANCE** Leaves in subtle colors like these look best in a simple arrangement. Here, a wide cement container holds branches arranged in the manner of a mixed floral bouquet.

# AUTUMN'S RICHES
## CELEBRATING FALL COLOR

*As the days grow shorter and the air gets nippy, many deciduous shrubs and trees begin their annual autumn show. Maple and sweet gum, oakleaf hydrangea and persimmon light up gardens and woodlands, dressed in colors that range from knockout bright to softer and subtler. The fall garden offers still more color and texture in the form of branches, berries, grasses, and seedpods. Head outside and look around: you'll find materials for arrangements that can dress up your home in wonderful ways.*

**EARTHEN TREASURES**
Displayed in a rustic unglazed pottery jug, this combination of tawny oakleaf hydrangea blooms, their colorful foliage, and clusters of red-blushed crabapples makes for a stunning arrangement. The casual, unstudied presentation lets the plants follow their natural habits; the hydrangeas spread generously above the jug's rim, while the heavy crabapples hang on their branches as they would on the tree. For advice on conditioning branches before putting them in water, see page 107.

**HIGH DRAMA** A study in line and form, this dramatic presentation gains its grandeur from a tall, spreading framework of blood red pokeweed stems. Feathery sprays of yellow goldenrod arch out and add fullness. An arrangement like this one is perfect for an entry hall, a stair landing, a front porch — anywhere you want to make an impressive statement.

**FANCY FORMS** Spider mums have an ornate, eye-catching form that makes for a fascinating all-of-a-kind bouquet. Pick them at various stages of maturity, from tightly furled buds to fully open blossoms; the contrast will create a lovely "work in progress." Mass the blossoms in a simple, understated container like this white ceramic urn.

# Marvelous Mums
## PRESENTING A PERENNIAL FALL FAVORITE

*It just wouldn't be fall without chrysanthemums, those versatile, colorful standbys for garden beds and bouquets. The best mums for cutting are the florists' type, available in a dizzying array of flower forms, sizes, and hues; you'll even find some multi-colored kinds.*

**STUDY IN SCARLET AND GOLD**
This stunning presentation stars classic anemone-form mums that offer a double dose of color: blushed red in the center, they shade to gold at the edges. Forming a jeweled collar around the flowers are plump, glossy blackberries—some still green, some beginning to ripen. A regal red-and-gold metal container completes a memorable picture. For tips on using metal containers, see page 25.

# ANNUALS

AGROSTEMMA GITHAGO. Corn cockle. Wispy, upright, 2- to 3-foot plant with grassy-looking leaves. Five-petaled, 2- to 3-inch-wide flowers are dark pink in the species, but named varieties have blossoms in purplish pink or white with purple markings. Species and varieties self-sow easily, but seedlings tend toward the basic dark pink. Needs only moderate water.

CELOSIA. Cockscomb. Three distinct flower types make good material for fresh or dried arrangements. Plume types have tiny flowers in large, plumelike clusters; crested types have bizarre-looking "rooster-comb" flower heads; so-called wheat types have slender blossom spikes. All grow as tall as 3 feet (with shorter varieties available) and come in brilliant shades of yellow, orange, red, pink, purple. Need only moderate water.

COREOPSIS TINCTORIA. Annual coreopsis. Narrow, upright, 1½- to 3-foot plant with 1½-inch daisies on wiry stems. Colors include yellow, orange, red, maroon, and bronze, usually banded with a contrasting color; flower centers are purplish brown. Double-flowered and shorter varieties are available. Needs only moderate water.

COSMOS BIPINNATUS. Leaves composed of many threadlike segments give this upright, branching, open plant a see-through quality. Yellow-centered, 3- to 4-inch-wide daisies on wiry stems come in white, lilac, pink, crimson, purple; petals of Seashell strain are rolled into a cone shape. Depending on the strain, height ranges from 1½ to 8 feet tall; Versailles strain, to 3½ feet, was developed especially for cutting. Needs only moderate water.

HELIANTHUS ANNUUS. Annual sunflower. In addition to the familiar big yellow type with a broad center and short petals, annual sunflowers now include smaller, shorter types in an expanded color range. These are compact, branching plants from 3½ to 8 feet tall, with single or double flowers ranging from 4 to 8 inches across. Best choices for cutting are those that don't shed pollen, among them the Large Flowered Mix and a number of named varieties in yellow, orange, red, bronze, bicolors. For best bloom, provide regular to ample water.

LAVATERA TRIMESTRIS. Annual mallow. Fast-growing, shrubby plant reaches 3 to 6 feet high and wide; named selections fall in the 2- to 4-foot range. Satiny, 4-inch flowers are circular in outline, with a prominent central spike of stamens. Colors include white, pink shades, rosy red. Remove spent flowers to keep bloom coming until frost.

SCABIOSA ATROPURPUREA. Pincushion flower. Slender, upright plants to 3 feet tall, with coarsely divided foliage and wiry stems supporting sweet-scented, 2- to 3-inch, slightly domed flower heads in white, blue, lavender, pink shades, crimson, blackish purple. Prominent stamens protrude from the flower heads, creating the "pincushion" look. Deadhead to keep bloom going until frost.

TAGETES. Marigold. Wide variety of choices in cream, yellow, gold, orange, maroon, mahogany. Most have double, pompomlike blooms, though some types have daisy-like single or semidouble flowers. All have finely divided, highly aromatic foliage. African marigold, *T. erecta*, comes in many named strains that range from 1½ to 3 feet tall, with flowers 3 to 5 inches across. French marigold, *T. patula*, has single, semidouble, and double blossoms in colors including rich mahogany tones; plants range from 6 to 18 inches high, flowers from 1 to 2½ inches wide. Hybrids between the two—the Triploid hybrids—look like larger versions of French marigolds. Deadhead all but the Triploid hybrids to prolong the flower show.

# SUMMER AND AUTUMN

*A few of these plants flower exclusively in fall, but most start their show during summer and keep on blooming until frost puts an end to the growing season. Unless otherwise noted, all need a sunny location, average to good soil, and regular watering; a few have special climate preferences. Hardiness—the lowest temperature at which the plant will survive—is stated for perennials and shrubs.*

*Helianthus annuus*

*Chrysanthemum*
*× morifolium*

*Gaillardia × grandiflora* 'Goblin'

TITHONIA ROTUNDIFOLIA. Mexican sunflower. Shrubby, coarse-textured plant reaches 6 feet high and 4 feet wide, blazing with orange-red, 4-inch daisies. Named varieties grow 2 to 4 feet tall and come in colors including yellow, gold, pure orange. Performs best where summers are hot.

ZINNIA ELEGANS. Upright plant with sandpapery leaves bears double daisies in bright, unshaded, unsubtle colors: yellow, orange, red, pink, lavender, purple, white, cream, even green ('Envy'). Some strains have blooms with quilled petals; others feature tufted centers surrounded by rows of flat petals. Plants range from 1 to 4 feet tall and bear flowers from 1 to 7 inches across. Zinnias revel in heat and dry air; they may suffer from mildew when air is moist.

## PERENNIALS AND BULBS

ASTER. New England aster, *A. novae-angliae,* and New York aster, *A. novi-belgii,* are mainstays of the fall garden. Both form dense clumps of upright, 3- to 5-foot stems bearing large, open clusters of 2-inch daisies. Blue violet is the basic color, but named selections come in white, rosy to wine red, and various shades of pink and blue; many of these have shorter stems than the species. Tallest kinds need staking to remain upright. Hardy to −30°F/−34°C.

CHRYSANTHEMUM × MORIFOLIUM. Florists' chrysanthemum. *The* fall flower, available in a dazzling assortment of forms, sizes, and colors. Only a trip to the nursery (or perusal of a specialty catalog) can do justice to the full array of choices. Borne on plants that vary from 1 to 3 feet high, flowers are all variations on the basic daisy—but they may be single, semidouble, or double, 1 inch to 8 inches wide, in forms including anemone, pompon, spider and many others—and in a color range including white, cream, yellow, orange, bronze, mahogany, red, pink, lavender, purple, and bicolors. Hardy to −20°F/−29°C.

CHRYSANTHEMUM × RUBELLUM. Finely divided leaves form a bushy foliage clump to 2½ feet high and wide, spangled at bloom time with 2- to 3-inch daisies. 'Clara Curtis' has bright pink flowers; those of 'Mary Stoker' are buff yellow. Hardy to −40°F/−40°C.

COREOPSIS ROSEA. Upright, branching plant to 2 feet tall, with narrow leaves and pink, 1-inch daisies. Hardy to −20°F/−29°C.

GAILLARDIA × GRANDIFLORA. Blanket flower. These hybrid daisies can reach 3 feet tall (the stems of dwarf forms are too short for cutting). Single to semidouble, 3- to 4-inch-wide flowers come in yellow or red shades, usually with concentric bands of orange or maroon and contrasting, often fringed petal tips. Needs moderate water; must have good drainage during winter. Hardy to −35°F/−37°C.

HELENIUM. Sneezeweed. Growing upright to 3 to 5 feet, the sneezeweeds produce 2- to 3-inch daisies in autumnal hues of yellow, orange, red, and mahogany, as well as combinations of these colors. Most widely available are hybrids (often sold—incorrectly—as selections of *H. autumnale).* Plants perform best where summers are hot. Hardy to −35°F/−37°C.

HELIANTHUS × MULTIFLORUS. Perennial sunflower. Plants in this hybrid group grow upright to 5 feet, with branching stems bearing 3-inch-wide, deep yellow flowers with yellow centers. Named selections include double-flowered 'Loddon Gold' ('Flore Pleno') and lemon yellow 'Capenoch Star', with a tufted, pincushion-like center. Hardy to −35°F/−37°C.

LILIUM. Lily. Like chrysanthemums, lilies offer so many different flower sizes, forms, colors, and color combinations that only a visit to a specialty grower (or catalog) can reveal the full spectrum of choices. All grow from bulbs, producing upright stems bearing elegant, often fragrant blossoms; height ranges from about 1½ to 8 feet. If you choose according to bloom time, you can enjoy lilies in flower throughout summer and into fall. Hardiness varies, but most prefer at least a little winter chill. Many are best in cool- to mild-summer regions and dislike the heat and humidity of the Deep South.

PHYSOSTEGIA VIRGINIANA. False dragonhead. Bushy plants clothed in narrow, toothed leaves may reach 4 feet high, 3 feet wide. Upright stems end in tapering spikes of cool pink, snapdragonlike flowers. Named varieties include 'Variegata', with cream-edged foliage, and selections with blooms in darker pink and white. Takes partial shade. Hardy to −35°F/−37°C.

SEDUM. Cut-flower candidates are *S. spectabile, S. telephium,* and *S.* 'Autumn Joy'. All form tight clumps of rubbery oval leaves that send up leafy, upright, 2-foot stems terminating in nearly flat-topped clusters of tiny, star-shaped blossoms. After blooms fade, the stems and flower clusters dry out (or can be gathered and dried) and look attractive in everlasting arrangements. 'Autumn Joy' has coppery pink blooms; selections of the other two species come in white, soft pink, rosy red, carmine red, and maroon. Hardy to −35°F/−37°C.

SOLIDAGO. Goldenrod. One of fall's harbingers, goldenrod is a narrow-leafed plant offering plumes and branching clusters of tiny yellow daisies on upright or arching stems that rise straight from the ground. Hybrid selections are improvements on wild forms. 'Goldenmosa' reaches 2½ feet tall; *S. rugosa* 'Fireworks' grows 4½ feet high and has arching stems and long sprays of golden flowers. Plants grow in sun or light shade, need only moderate water. Hardy to −40°F/−40°C.

STOKESIA LAEVIS. Stokes aster. Their petals are so heavily fringed that these double daisies look like bachelor's buttons. Clumps of linear leaves send up stems to 2 feet tall bearing light lavender-blue, 3- to 4-inch blooms; named selections come in white, pink, purple. Blooms intermittently all year in mild-winter regions. Hardy to −20°F/−29°C.

*Physostegia virginiana*

*Sedum* 'Autumn Joy'

# EVERLASTING ARRANGEMENTS

*The blooms in your garden come and go all too quickly, often leaving you wishing that their fleeting beauty could be prolonged. Good news: by drying and preserving your favorites, you can savor their lovely colors and forms throughout the year—and to add to the pleasure, you can freely mix elements of many kinds, from different seasons. The very simple air-drying method lets you preserve such flowers as baby's breath, cockscomb, Chinese lantern, cupid's dart, hydrangea, larkspur, lavender, statice, yarrow, and many more. (For a complete list of plant selections and for drying tips, see pages 112–113.) Other plant materials can also be dried for use in arrangements; try herb leaves, ornamental grasses, seedpods, and berries.*

When arranging dried flowers, follow the general advice on color, form, and design we give in this book for fresh flowers. Keep in mind, though, that dried flowers often have softer, subtler colors than their fresh counterparts. A good example is the bouquet of dried hydrangeas shown on the facing page: the colors have softened to smoky, subtle hues that harmonize beautifully with stems of dried lavender (statice and larkspur would also look attractive).

Because dried arrangements don't need water, your options for containers are incredibly varied. Do, however, select those with quiet colors and materials that will complement rather than overwhelm the flowers. Baskets are a particularly good choice. You can also use vases, decorative tins, and terra-cotta pots.

The lack of dependence on water also makes dried flowers ideal candidates for wreaths, nosegays, and other decorations that would have a much shorter life if made with fresh flowers. The nosegay shown at right is particularly easy to assemble, and it makes a charming dinner-party favor. Simply select a harmonious grouping of flowers and leaves, take two or three stems of each (cut to about 3 inches long), and tie the bunch with raffia. Here, we've used purple and white statice along with fresh camellia leaves; other choices might include baby's breath, globe amaranth, lavender, or yarrow with fresh citrus leaves or with sword or maidenhair ferns.

Here are a few tips for arranging dried flowers.

- Handle dried flowers carefully; many are brittle and can shatter easily.

- Just before arranging the flowers, recondition them by spraying lightly with water to make them more pliable.

- Use floral foam to anchor stems. If the container permits, you can use fine, clean sand as an alternative anchor.

- Spray finished arrangements with aerosol hairspray to protect them.

- If arrangements get dusty, clean them with a gentle stream of air from a blow dryer on a cool setting.

**FLOWERS AFLOAT** Some winter blossoms, like these stunning camellias, have such short stems that displaying them in a vase is difficult. But floating them in a wide, shallow bowl shows off their beauty dramatically. A glossy leaf or two adds contrast and interest to the composition.

# WINTER BLOSSOMS
## SHOWCASING THE DELICATE
## BEAUTY OF MILD-WINTER FLOWERS

WINTER

*If you live in an area where winters are mild, you can grow shrubs, trees, and even some perennials and cool-season annuals that yield lovely flowers for winter arrangements. Check the lists on pages 90–91 for ideas. And don't forget that the winter garden also offers handsome foliage—leaves and branches that can serve either as an arrangement's main focus or as an accent or filler in a floral composition.*

**WINTER WHITE** At first glance, you might not recognize these lavishly ruffled blooms: after all, cyclamens don't immediately spring to mind as candidates for cut-flower arrangements. But gathered in a little glass vase that's narrow enough to hold the tender stems upright, they look utterly charming. The large-flowered cyclamens shown here are florists' cyclamens, typically sold in pots during cool-weather times of year.

**HANDSOME HELLEBORES** Though hellebores have been overlooked in the past as cut flowers, their subtle hues and delicate markings make them delightful in bouquets. These easy-to-grow plants include the familiar Lenten rose and Christmas rose, both of which come into bloom in winter. Here, the blossoms are displayed in a gleaming ceramic vase that plays up their unusual colors and transforms what might look a bit subdued into an eye-catching presentation. Vase by Katrine Benninger.

**BOUQUET OF SUNSHINE** In late winter, nothing can match a bouquet of frothy acacia for cheering up a room. The feathery foliage on the branches adds to the arrangement's lushness. Here, a tall, trumpet-shaped ceramic vase combines with the spreading branches to give the composition a natural fan shape. *Note:* Acacia pollen is dry and usually can be removed from most surfaces by blowing on it gently (don't brush it, or it will smear). To avoid any possibility of staining, however, keep it off your most valuable soft furnishings. One other caution—don't bring acacia indoors if you're allergic to it!

### APPLE BLOSSOM TIME
Spangled on delicate stems, apple blossoms rise gracefully above the vase. The tall, straight cuttings look best arranged in a natural manner; crisscross the dark stems as you insert them into the container, and you'll easily achieve a loose fan shape. The sky blue glass vase in our arrangement both shows off the stems and amplifies the pale winter light shining through the window.

### STATELY QUINCE
Blooming on bare branches in winter, flowering quince offers breathtaking beauty outdoors and in. Shown here are blossoms in softest blush pink, but you'll find varieties in a colors ranging from white to bright pink to tomato red. Here, we used a plump, creamy container that complements the tall stems and harmonizes with the delicate color of the flowers.

# HINTS OF SPRING
## BUDDING BRANCHES USHER IN SPRING AHEAD OF SCHEDULE

*Outdoors, it may still be late winter—but inside, you can get a headstart on spring by cutting and forcing the branches of spring-blossoming trees and shrubs. Among the many candidates for this treatment are flowering quince, forsythia, and many fruit trees, including apple, apricot, cherry, and peach. Take cuttings when the first buds are just showing color or have barely opened. Indoors, they'll continue to unfurl as they would on the tree—but more quickly. When you cut, always use proper pruning practices, cutting back to a side branch or growth bud. (Don't just clip off branches randomly; this may leave stubs that will eventually die.) Before you arrange the branches, slit the ends or pound them with a hammer to spread the fibers (see page 107). This allows them to continue taking up water once in the container.*

# HOME FOR THE HOLIDAYS

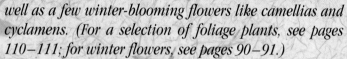

*With their deep green color and spicy fragrance, evergreens are a classic choice for dressing up your home during the winter holidays—and they're available in almost every climate. The branches of evergreens like spruce, cedar, pine, fir, juniper, and redwood are beautiful both on their own and as foils for all sorts of decorative accessories, from candles to ornaments. Glossy citrus and magnolia leaves, variegated foliage of some hollies, and colorful winter berries provide natural accents. In mild-winter climates, garden selections expand to include even more evergreen trees and shrubs, as well as a few winter-blooming flowers like camellias and cyclamens. (For a selection of foliage plants, see pages 110–111; for winter flowers, see pages 90–91.)*

GATHERING GREENS. Try this trick. A week before cutting, mark the branches you want with pieces of twine or ribbon. Then mix a solution of 1 to 2 tablespoons Epsom salts to 1 gallon water; fill a spray bottle with it and spray your chosen branches. The magnesium in the salts will intensify leaf color and luster. When you cut your evergreens, cut back to side branches or growth buds; don't just clip randomly, or you may leave stubs that will eventually die. To help branches absorb water and thus last longer, slit the ends or pound them with a hammer (see page 107). Soak them in water overnight, foliage and all; then hang them the next day to straighten and dry.

CREATIVE ARRANGEMENTS. On these pages, we show several fresh holiday arrangements you might want to try. For creating these and other compositions, you'll find floral foam a highly useful tool. A block of foam, soaked in water and then drained, forms the base for the simplest arrangement—fir and cedar boughs heaped in a silver ice bucket and topped with an assortment of gleaming tree ornaments (right).

The centerpiece in the footed silver dish (below), as aromatic as it is lovely to look at, includes cedar and eucalyptus cuttings, pepper berries, and large sugar-pine cones. Two moistened blocks of floral foam form the base. We used a knife to carve out small hollows in the foam; the pinecones were set into these, so they appear to be nestled down into the greenery. The cuttings were then inserted into the foam; finally, the whole arrangement was topped with a length of wired silk ribbon.

The candle centerpiece (facing page, top) was made using a floral foam ring in its own plastic dish (available from craft and hobby stores, florists' suppliers, or flower markets). After the foam was soaked and drained, cuttings of pine, cedar, and holly were inserted into it. The ring of greenery wreathes a collection of pillar candles in various sizes. For added protection for your tabletop, you may want to underlay the entire arrangement with a shallow-rimmed tray or a sheet of plastic.

# WINTER

*Even winter has its share of flowers, though these are available only to gardeners in largely snow-free climates. Where winters are cold and potentially snowy, the annuals and the hardy perennials and shrubs described here will bloom in early spring. Unless otherwise noted, all need a sunny spot, average to good soil, and regular watering; a few have special climate preferences. Hardiness— the minimum winter temperature a plant will tolerate—is noted for all but annuals.*

*Papaver nudicale*

## ANNUALS

ANTIRRHINUM MAJUS. Snapdragon. See "Spring" (page 48).

CALENDULA OFFICINALIS. Semidouble to double, 2½- to 4½-inch daisies are borne on individual stems. Colors include cream, yellow, orange, and apricot. Branching, somewhat sprawling plants have aromatic, slightly sticky stems and leaves. Some strains reach 2 feet high and wide; dwarfs are half that size.

LATHYRUS ODORATUS. Sweet pea. See "Spring" (page 48).

MATTHIOLA INCANA. Stock. See "Spring" (page 48).

MYOSOTIS SYLVATICA. Forget-me-not. Soft, hairy leaves cover a bushy plant to 1 foot high and twice as wide. Small clusters of little flowers are spangled over the plant; typical color is pure blue with a white eye, but all-white and lilac-pink forms are available. Self-sows profusely.

PAPAVER NUDICAULE. Iceland poppy. Clumps of hairy leaves send up needle-thin, 1- to 2-foot stems, each bearing a single satiny, bowl-shaped flower to 3 inches across. Colors include white, cream, and pastel to bright shades of pink, salmon, orange, and red.

PRIMULA MALACOIDES. Fairy primrose. Tight clumps of oval, long-stalked leaves send up 8- to 15-inch stems bearing tiered whorls of 1-inch flowers in white, lavender, pink, and rosy red.

VIOLA. Pansy, viola. See "Spring" (page 48).

## PERENNIALS AND BULBS

BERGENIA. Both flowers and foliage are attractive in arrangements. Long-stalked, rubbery-textured leaves are oval to paddle shaped, to about 8 inches long; clumps reach 1½ feet high. Thick flower stems bear nodding clusters of blossoms shaped like open bells; colors include pink shades, white, rose red, and magenta. *B. cordifolia, B. crassifolia,* and numerous named hybrids are available. Hardy to −30°F/−34°C.

EUPHORBIA. Spurge. Two winter-blooming spurges have upright stems that are thickly clothed with linear gray-green leaves, giving them the look of bottlebrushes. Tiny flowers are held in cup-shaped chartreuse bracts arranged in open, dome-shaped clusters at stem ends. *E. characias wulfenii (E. veneta)* reaches 4 feet high; *E. × martinii* grows 2 to 3 feet tall. Hardy to 5°F/−15°C.

HELLEBORUS. Mounded, foot-tall foliage clumps consist of long-stalked leaves with narrowly oval leaflets arranged like the outstretched fingers of a hand. Flowers are cup or saucer shaped, 2 to 3 inches across. Christmas rose, *H. niger,* has white blossoms that age to purplish pink; it needs winter chill. Lenten rose, *H. orientalis,* and its hybrids do not need winter chill and bloom a bit later than *H. niger.* Colors range from greenish or buff-tinted white through pinkish tones to maroon and purple; blossoms frequently show dark spots or freckling. Both Christmas and Lenten rose are hardy to −30°F/−34°C.

NARCISSUS. Daffodil, narcissus. Long, narrow, strap-shaped leaves grow from bulbs. Flowers have a distinctive shape, with a cup or trumpet resting on a circular "ruff" of petals. Stems typically are 8 to 16 inches high. Basic colors are white and yellow, but there are many bicolors featuring either of these two colors plus orange, red, or pink. Types known as narcissus have clusters of 1- to 2-inch flowers and are hardy to around 10°F/−12°C. Those called daffodils generally have one 2- to 4-inch flower per stem and bloom a bit later than narcissus. Hardy to −30°F/−34°C.

PRIMULA × POLYANTHA. Polyanthus primrose. Clumps of tongue-shaped, lettuce-like leaves send up 8- to 12-inch stems bearing clusters of scallop-edged, circular blossoms to 2 inches across. Colors include all but black and true green; flowers usually have yellow centers. Hardy to −30°F/−34°C.

VIOLA ODORATA. Sweet violet. Wide-spreading clumps to 8 inches high, composed of long-stalked, nearly circular leaves. Inch-wide blossoms with a distinctive perfume come on stems that rise just above the leaves. Colors include purple, lavender, blue, white, pink. Hardy to −30°F/−34°C.

## SHRUBS

CAMELLIA JAPONICA. Evergreen. Glossy, broadly oval dark green leaves clothe plants growing 6 to 12 feet (possibly as tall as 20 feet) high. Single to double flowers (including several specialty forms) come in white, pink, red, many variegated combinations; size runs from 2 to 6 inches across. Bloom time depends on variety: some flower in December, others as late as March. Prefers partial to full shade. Hardy to about 0°F/−18°C.

CHAENOMELES. Flowering quince. Deciduous. Dense, bulky, upright shrubs reach 10 feet or more, spread half as wide as high; most are somewhat thorny. Twiggy bare branches are studded with single or semidouble, 1½- to 2½-inch flowers in white, pink shades, coral, orange, red. Hardy to −30°F/−34°C.

CHIMONANTHUS PRAECOX. Wintersweet. Deciduous. Upright, many-stemmed plant produces small clusters of pale yellow, spicy-scented, inch-wide flowers on bare stems. Hardy to 0°F/−18°C.

ERICA. Heath. Evergreen. Many species, from spreading ground covers to shrub-trees; most have small, urn-shaped flowers in dense clusters. Standard colors are white, pink, red, purple, and lilac. Plants need moist, cool air. Northern European types grow in mid-Atlantic, Northeastern, southern Great Lakes, and Pacific Coast regions; Mediterranean and South African types grow only in the Pacific Coast states. Hardiness varies with the species or variety.

EUPHORBIA PULCHERRIMA. Poinsettia. Evergreen. The familiar December holiday flower, originally only in red but now including white, cream, pink, and variegated forms. Big, rangy plant has large, broadly toothed leaves; the tiny true flowers are surrounded by large, colorful bracts that pass for petals. In the garden, plants usually bloom in January, February. Hardy to 20°F/−7°C.

FORSYTHIA. Deciduous. Upright to fountainlike, 6- to 10-foot plants bear profuse bell-shaped brilliant yellow flowers on bare branches. *F. × intermedia* selections are hardy to −20°F/−29°C; several hardy hybrids—including 'Meadow Lark', 'New Hampshire Gold', and 'Northern Sun'—are hardy to −30°F/−34°C.

HAMAMELIS. Witch hazel. Deciduous. Large shrubs reach 12 to 15 feet high and wide. Bare branches are decorated in clusters of fragrant flowers that look like shredded coconut; named varieties come in yellow, orange, coppery red orange. *H. × intermedia* varieties, *H. japonica* (Japanese witch hazel), and *H. mollis* (Chinese witch hazel) are hardy to −20°F/−29°C. *H. vernalis* (Ozark witch hazel) and *H. virginiana* (common witch hazel) are hardy to −30°F/−34°C.

*Helleborus orientalis*

*Forsythia × intermedia*

# GARDENS FOR
# CUT FLOWERS

*It's often easier to imagine the arrangements and bouquets you want to create than it is to visualize the garden where the flowers and foliage will grow. Plants raised commercially for cutting are mass-produced in field rows and green-houses—options hardly available to the average homeowner. Still, the home garden offers several approaches to growing flowers, foliage, and branches to use for indoor arrangements.*

*In this chapter, we guide you through the establishment and care of cutting gardens—from choosing the kind of garden suited to your needs and preparing it for planting, to providing routine care and, finally, gathering the beautiful harvest. Separate sections highlight specialty plants—roses, flowers for drying, and sorts grown for decorative leaves, berries, or branches. The final 12 pages present sketches and plot plans for gardens that will deliver cut materials to suit a variety of needs.*

This well-tended cutting garden bursts with summer bloom
from cosmos, yarrow, dahlias, sunflowers, and more.

# WHAT KIND OF CUTTING GARDEN?

*When you're establishing a cutting garden, don't just charge outside with a shovel and some seed packets—take the time to plan. Once you've decided what you need, the outdoor work can begin.*

Start by asking yourself a few questions. Will you be happy with flowers alone, or do you also want other material: foliage, berries, attractive twigs and branches? What time of year should material be available? Some gardeners focus on spring and/or summer, while others want something for cutting all year round. Note that if you're interested largely in floral displays for spring and summer, you'll find many dozens of plant choices. Fall- and winter-blooming plants are less numerous, though—so if you want late-in-the-year arrangements, you're likely to need more than just flowers.

Also consider how much room you can devote to a cutting garden. If space is limited, choose plants with the longest possible bloom periods in order to get the most from the available ground. Note, too, that if you have virtually *no* space for a separate cutting garden, you can always work the plants into the general landscape: the flowers, foliage, berries, and/or branches they offer for arrangements will come as a bonus.

## LOCATION AND LAYOUT

As is true for other plantings, success comes from choosing plants whose needs are met by the conditions you already have or can easily create.

SITING THE BED. On a small property, there may be no question as to where the cutting garden should go: you put it wherever a spot is open! When you have a choice of locations, however, think about convenience. All other things being equal, it's best to site the planting close enough to the house to let you visit it easily and often, so you can dart out quickly to gather materials for a last-minute arrangement. A bed closer to the house is also more likely to get timely maintenance, even something as basic as watering.

EXPOSURE. The majority of cut-flower plants need plenty of sun. Depending on the climate, though, you may need to moderate the exposure a bit. Where summers are blazing hot, even sun lovers often appreciate a little light afternoon shade (the equivalent of an overcast sky) to save them from roasting during the hottest part of the day. But where summers are cool to mild and skies are often cloudy, most sun-loving plants—particularly summer bloomers—need a spot that receives day-long sun when weather is clear. Even on gray days, plants in such a location will get the greatest amount of light available.

Be aware of changing light patterns during the growing season. The sun's height in the sky increases as the year progresses toward the summer solstice, then decreases from that date until the start of winter. Thus, the bed that enjoys total sunlight in summer may not be sunny at all for part of spring or fall. When planting sun-loving spring flowers, be sure to choose a spot that will be sunny at the right time.

What if your only available site is in full or partial shade the year around? You can still grow a cutting garden there—but you'll need to select only plants that prefer these dimmer conditions, such as astilbe, campanula, and hellebore.

BED LAYOUT. Among possible garden designs, the "factory" style, with plants in rows or blocks, is the most efficient (an important consideration when space is tight) and delivers the most bloom for the space. It's planted according to the concept of the traditional vegetable garden, though of course the crop is floral rather than edible. If you prefer to avoid the "flower farm" setup, you can go for a more informal style, as in our summer island beds (pages 118–119).

Whatever the layout, it goes without saying that the plants should be easy to reach, since you'll be gathering their blooms frequently. Though you can always step into a bed to cut flowers or do maintenance, the most convenient plantings are those that allow ready access from the outside. For a planting with one open side, 3 to 4 feet is about the maximum depth for easy picking; for beds accessible from either side, a width of about 7 feet is the limit for convenient harvesting.

Within a planting, pay attention to ultimate plant heights. Cutting is easiest when you locate the shortest plants at the front, the tallest ones in the rear. That's usually the preferred arrangement for peak plant performance, too, since it prevents larger plants from shading out smaller individuals.

If you set up a bed open on all sides in full sun, consider its alignment to the sun's daily path across the sky. Take a tip from vegetable growers: align beds (and rows, if you use them) in a north-south direction, so that the sun, in its east-west trajectory, delivers equal amounts of light to all parts of the planting. Locating the tallest plants on the north side or end will keep them from shading the shorter plants in the bed.

## CHOOSING THE PLANTS

For cut flowers, you want production—so cooperate with Mother Nature. Choose the plants that will grow and bloom easily in your climate (Kansas is for sunflowers, not tropical orchids) or in conditions you can create with some modifications. Note that those modifications should be relatively minor; you probably don't want to alter the native conditions extensively just to coax a precious crop from fussy exotics. Delphiniums, for example, revel in the coolness of the Northwest and northern latitudes. Growing them in warmer and/or drier regions is an increasing challenge until you reach points in the steamy Deep South and the arid Southwest where the results, if any, are so pathetic that the struggle isn't worth the effort.

The plant descriptions in the preceding chapter highlight climate preferences, where applicable, and indicate the cold tolerance (survivable low temperatures) for perennials and woody plants. For additional information on these plants and thousands more, consult any of the *Sunset* regional garden books (for the West, Midwest, or Northeast) or the *Southern Living Garden Book.*

Beyond considering a plant's adaptability to local conditions, think about its general category—annual, perennial, flowering shrub, and so on. Annual plants complete their life cycle within a single growing season, while more permanent perennials, bulbs, and shrubs return year after year, needing only periodic maintenance such as division or pruning. Each group has its pros and cons.

A cottage-style cutting garden, brimming with potential bouquets

*Cosmos bipinnatus* (annual)

ᗡ **Annuals** This group of plants includes the individuals that give you the most floral bounty for your money and space. Marigolds, to cite one ubiquitous example, knock themselves out with bloom from late spring into fall, starting from seeds or young plants planted in early spring. But when the growing season ends, they die. The next year, you must replant—and, ideally, replenish the supply of organic matter and nutrients in the soil. Thus, though annuals may give you the greatest rewards, they also obligate you to the same start-from-scratch work…annually.

TOP: *Achillea millefolium* (yarrow; perennial)
MIDDLE: *Chaenomeles* (flowering quince; shrub)
BOTTOM: *Rosa* 'Gold Medal' (grandiflora rose; shrub)

🙝 **Perennials** These plants vary widely in appearance and season of bloom. Some, like blanket flower *(Gaillardia × grandiflora),* have flowering periods virtually equal to those of long-blooming annuals. Others, like peonies and irises, make one grand statement over a few weeks' time, then take a break until next year. That's for *flowering* perennials. But these plants also include a number that give you foliage for arrangements—leaves that may be available from spring through fall.

Some perennials (peonies are the perfect example) can remain in place for years if not decades, needing only minimal annual care—an application of fertilizer in early spring, cleanup of spent leaves and stems in autumn. Others form clumps that decline in performance as they become crowded; these must be divided every several years to maintain abundant, good-quality bloom. And some just peter out after a while and need to be replaced with new plants raised from cuttings or obtained from a nursery.

🙝 **Shrubs** These woody plants may give you a lifetime of flowers and foliage from an initial planting. Remember, though, that most bloom at just one time of year, then remain leafy for the duration of the growing season (evergreen shrubs stay leafy all year round). If the foliage is also good for arrangements, or if the blooms are followed by decorative fruits, the plant really pays for its space. If only the blossoms are usable in arrangements, however, think twice about putting the plant in a cutting garden. A general garden location might be more appropriate, freeing cutting-garden space for more productive choices.

Among shrubs, roses merit special attention. They're the notable exception to the once-a-year bloom rule: modern repeat-flowering kinds give you blossoms from spring through summer and on into fall, for as long as your climate permits. Where space allows, many gardeners devote entire beds—even entire gardens—exclusively to roses (see pages 108–109).

## SOIL SAVVY

Though some shrubs are indifferent to soil quality, most cut-flower annuals and perennials need average or better soil for peak performance. Before you plant, learn a little about your soil and take the time to prepare it thoroughly; the effort will really pay off. Especially for annuals (but for many perennials, too), the vegetable-garden parallel holds: good soil leads to good crops.

SOIL TYPE. If a plant is to grow well, its roots must have adequate water, air, and nutrients. How well these needs are met—independent of any contribution by the gardener—depends in part on soil type.

Soils vary from heavy, dense clay at one extreme to light, porous sand at the other. *Clay soils* are composed of tiny, flattened mineral particles that pack closely together. Water enters such soils slowly and percolates through them equally slowly, keeping roots moist and maintaining dissolved nutrients longer. The down side is that roots have a hard time penetrating clay, and they can literally suffocate if too much water is applied. *Sandy soils,* in contrast, are loose in texture, composed of rounded, relatively large particles. Roots grow easily in sand, but water and dissolved nutrients move through so rapidly that, without adequate attention to watering and fertilizing, plants in sandy soil may be spindly and undergrown. Most garden soils fall somewhere between the two extremes of clay and sand, but you'll probably be able to identify yours as more like one or the other—and care for your plants accordingly.

Soils are, of course, more than mineral particles, water, and air. *Organic matter*—the decomposing remains of formerly living material—is the dynamic ingredient that makes soils "better." Be it homemade compost or a commercial product, organic matter improves any soil. Lodging between particles and particle groups, it loosens clay (thus speeding up drainage) and acts like water-retentive sponge in sand. Root growth is better in amended soil, and vigorous root growth pays dividends above ground. For this reason, adding plenty of organic matter prior to planting is always a valuable first step toward great results later on.

SOIL PREPARATION. If weeds or vegetables flourish in your soil, it may also give you good cut-flower results for a year or two at least. But even if soil is good, you can improve your crop by preparing your planting areas—that is, by digging or rotary tilling in organic matter and fertilizer. As noted above, organic matter improves or enhances soil structure, while fertilizer ensures that key nutrients will be available to the plants you'll set out later.

Start with a rough assessment of your soil. If it is fairly clay-like or on the sandy side, it will benefit from more rather than less organic matter. Compost is the classic organic amendment, but having enough on hand requires advance planning. Most gardeners, at least initially, purchase organic materials in bags or bales at nurseries and garden supply outlets; gardeners in agricultural areas may have access to crop by-products that, when partially decomposed, make good and fairly inexpensive amendments. Commercially packaged products may contain animal manures, wood by-products, rice hulls, processed feathers, and so on, as well as materials such as ground oyster shells to add calcium.

Wood by-products (such as chips and sawdust) are particularly good amendments for clay soils, since they physically loosen the structure but do not hold moisture. When using such products, however, always check the label to make sure nitrogen has been added to aid in decomposition ("nitrogen stabilized" and "nitrogen fortified" are two standard phrases). Without added nitrogen, wood by-products will extract nitrogen from the soil, competing with plant roots.

Among fertilizers, look for a dry complete product (see page 103) that contains some nitrogen but greater percentages of phosphorus and potassium—a 5-10-10 formula, for example. It's important to apply a good dose of the latter two nutrients at root level, where plants can use them; they are not water soluble and will not move through the soil if applied at the surface, but once incorporated in a bed they remain available to roots for a fairly long period. Nitrogen, in contrast, is water soluble: it leaches out of the soil over the growing season, but you can reapply it at the surface as needed. It will move downward and be absorbed by plant roots.

To prepare soil for planting, start by clearing away all weeds. If the soil isn't easy to dig, water it thoroughly; then let it dry until it's moist. It should be easy to work but no longer wet. Dig or till it to a depth of 10 to 12 inches, breaking up clods and removing any debris such as old roots and large stones. Rake it to re-establish a roughly level surface.

Next, scatter on fertilizer in the amount the package directs; then spread on organic amendments (as well as any materials recommended to adjust pH). A 3- to 4-inch layer of organic material worked into 12 inches of soil is ideal, guaranteed to create a hospitable root run. But any lesser amount is better than none at all. As a rule of thumb, figure that a cubic yard of any organic material will cover 100 square feet (a 5- by 20-foot bed, for example) to a depth of 3 inches. Dig or till the soil to the depth you initially worked it, thoroughly incorporating all amendments; then rake it level and water it well. If possible, let a week or more pass before you plant.

## ACID OR ALKALINE?

Any soil can be rated according to the pH (potential hydrogen) scale. Soils with a pH of 7 are neutral, neither acid nor alkaline; those with a pH below 7 are acidic, while those with a pH above 7 are alkaline. Many plants grow well in soils ranging from moderately acid to slightly alkaline, though some popular woody sorts such as rhododendron and heather need soil on the acid side. When pH is extreme in either direction, however, certain nutrients needed for root growth become chemically "tied up," unavailable to plant roots; only a few especially tolerant plants thrive under such conditions. Highly acidic soils tend to be found in higher-rainfall areas, while notably alkaline soils are more common to arid and semiarid regions of the Southwest. If you suspect that your soil is strongly acid or alkaline, contact your Cooperative Extension Office or county farm advisor for advice and possible remedies. A soil testing lab will (for a fee) perform the same services; look in the Yellow Pages under "Soil Laboratories."

# RAISED BEDS

*A raised bed is just what the name implies: a planting bed elevated 8 to 12 inches above grade. In its most basic form, it's simply a raised plateau of soil. More often, though, you'll encounter raised beds surrounded by a low "wall" of wood (such as 2-inch-thick lumber or railroad ties), concrete, brick, or stone.*

Though making a raised bed does take a bit of effort, it gives you a number of advantages. If you have problem soil—impenetrable clay, nutrient-deficient sand, a soil that's highly acid or alkaline or one that's compacted from construction—a raised bed filled with good soil may be your best shot at raising healthy plants. (Particularly where drainage is slow to nonexistent, a raised bed is the easiest way to provide a well-drained root run.) And even if your garden soil is good enough for what you want to grow, a raised bed may be worth installing: it will help you prepare a "powerhouse" plot for top production, a defined area where you can add topsoil, amendments, and fertilizer to make the finest possible soil.

In cold-winter regions, soil in raised beds warms earlier than that in regular garden plots, allowing you to plant and harvest earlier as well. When it comes time to pick the flowers, the elevated soil level makes the job a bit simpler. And the fact that plants and soil are contained makes the entire operation neat and tidy: water and fertilizer (and soil) remain within the bed.

When planning a raised bed, choose the site carefully. Most cut-flower plants are sun loving, so the bed should receive at least 6 hours of sun daily. Select a spot that has good air circulation but is not exposed to frequent winds. Be sure, too, to locate it at some distance from trees and large shrubs; if they're too close, their roots will infiltrate the soil of the bed. Also make sure that a hose bibb or other water source is near enough to make watering easy.

To the extent that you can, loosen up the soil where the raised bed will be. This way, you'll be able to mix the existing soil with whatever you use to fill the bed, creating some transition between the native soil and that of the bed. And of course, loosening the soil below the bed will make it easier for roots to penetrate as deeply as possible.

Now you're ready to build the bed. No matter what material you use as a border, the base should extend about 2 inches below soil level. If you construct a wood frame (see facing page), you can assemble it off-site and move it into place. Dimensions are important: you should be able to reach into the bed's center easily from either side.

With the border in place, you can fill the bed with additional soil. If your soil is good, you might just add soil from somewhere else in the garden. Another option is to use purchased topsoil (be aware, though, that this product varies greatly, depending on the supplier—some topsoils are raw dirt, while others are mixtures of soil and organic amendments). Fill the bed in stages: add several inches of new soil and dig it into the native soil beneath; then add several more inches and dig it into the previously dug soil. Spread organic amendments over the soil and sprinkle on fertilizer (if needed), then dig these in thoroughly. The settled level of the finished bed should be about 2 inches below the top edge of the border.

## SCREENING OUT GOPHERS

If pocket gophers are a serious problem in your area, consider a screen-bottomed bed that will prevent them from getting to your plants. Make a wooden framework as shown on the facing page; then staple $3/16$-inch-mesh hardware cloth to the bottom before setting the frame into the soil. Be aware that you must dig quite carefully in screen-bottomed beds; and of course, you can't dig below the depth of the bed. For this reason, it's best to make these beds a bit deeper—up to $1\frac{1}{2}$ feet.

STEP 1: Cut 2 by 6 lumber and 4 by 4 end- and midposts to length. Use an electric drill to make pilot holes for nails or screws.

STEP 2: After attaching boards for one end, set that section upright. Then nail or screw on boards for side of bed, being sure side boards cover butt ends of end boards.

STEP 3: When bed is fully assembled, it's ready to set in place. Before you install it, loosen the soil and dig shallow trenches for recessing the sides.

STEP 4: Use a shovel to dig and fill as needed, to adjust bed's position in the soil. Use a carpenter's level to ensure that finished bed will be level.

STEP 5: After bed is in place and leveled, use a sledgehammer to drive ½-inch steel stake up against each side and end to anchor bed in place.

STEP 6: For a finished appearance, cap the bed with 2 by 6 finished lumber. Miter the corners; then use an electric drill to make pilot holes for nails or screws.

# Planting Techniques

*Annuals and perennials form the backbone of the cut-flower garden, and any well-stocked nursery or garden center will offer an ample selection of young plants ready to set out. For instructions on planting these, see page 102. Sometimes, though, you'll want to start from seed—to get the jump on the growing season, to grow less-common plants or special varieties, or just for the joy of the process.*

## RAISING PLANTS FROM SEED

When planting seeds, you have a choice of two methods. You can sow them directly in the ground where they'll grow to maturity, or you can start them in containers for planting out at a later date. The technique you choose will depend on your climate and on the plants you intend to grow.

SOWING SEEDS IN CONTAINERS. Though it requires a bit more labor than in-ground planting, starting seeds in containers is the method of choice for most gardeners. For plants with seeds that are dust-fine or slow to germinate, containers offer the safest nursery. And in colder-winter regions with short growing seasons, starting seeds of frost-tender annuals indoors gives you plants to set outdoors at the earliest possible frost-free moment—so you'll get flowers earlier, too. Seedlings growing in containers are also easier to protect from predatory creatures (birds included) during the vulnerable early stages of development.

Suitable containers for seed-starting include flats, clay pots, plastic nursery pots, cell-packs that once held nursery plants, styrofoam cups, and more. Make sure the containers you use have a drainage hole or holes; before use, clean them thoroughly to remove old soil and any disease organisms. Fill the containers with a soil mix that is moisture retentive but porous: it should hold water well enough to encourage the seedlings' hair-fine roots but drain fast enough to avoid becoming waterlogged. Ordinary garden soil, even if liberally amended with organic matter, is too dense for container

### SOWING IN FLATS

Plastic foam flat contains individual cells. Plant two seeds to a cell; later thin seedlings to one per cell. As plants grow, move them to individual pots.

### SOWING IN SMALL CONTAINERS

STEP 1: Sow seeds in container of potting mix; scatter them so that seedlings won't be too crowded. Cover with mix to the appropriate depth.

STEP 2: When seedlings have their second set of true leaves, gently knock them out of the container.

STEP 3: Separate seedlings. Fill small containers with potting soil; replant seedlings individually.

use; it forms a solid mass that roots cannot penetrate easily, and it remains soggy for too long after watering. A better bet is one of the packaged potting mixes sold at nurseries and garden centers.

Plant the seeds as shown in the photos on the facing page. When they have germinated, set containers where light is ample and bright; a sunny window or greenhouse is ideal. When the seedlings have their second set of true leaves, transplant them from their pots to individual containers or cells of soil as shown in the photos.

Place the transplanted seedlings in a location with bright light. Water them regularly; apply half-strength liquid fertilizer weekly. About 10 days before you intend to plant the seedlings in the garden, start preparing them for the transition. Stop fertilizing, and set the plants outside in a wind-sheltered location for several hours each day. For the first several days, place them in filtered sunlight. Then, over the course of a week or so, gradually increase their exposure to sunlight so that, by the end of the 10-day conditioning period, they can endure a full day's sunshine. At that point, you can plant them in their garden beds.

DIRECT SOWING. Most of the seeds you can start in containers can also be sown directly in the ground. And where the growing season is long, there's no need to start frost-tender plants indoors to achieve early bloom; in these regions, you can plant early both indoors and out. Some plants, however, are usually raised in any climate from seeds sown directly where they are to grow. These include plants with large, easy-to-plant seeds and those with carrotlike taproots that resent disturbance.

For direct sowing, prepare the soil as described on page 97, paying special attention to leveling and smoothing it once amendment is complete. Water the prepared ground, relevel it if needed, and water again. You can sow seeds in rows, plant them in blocks, or even broadcast them. Row planting is simplest. You space rows as far apart as the mature plants should be (as stated on the seed packet); when the seedlings have their second set of true leaves, you thin them to the proper spacing within the rows. With block planting, you try to space seeds the correct distance apart in all directions; for broadcasting (shown at right) you sow them liberally over the area, then thin the seedlings as needed.

No matter how you plant your seeds, bury them only as deep as the packet recommends; a good rule of thumb is to plant twice as deep as the seed is thick. Keep the seed bed evenly moist but not saturated until germination is complete. When the young plants have two or three sets of true leaves, you can cut back slightly on watering; the root zone should always be moist, but the soil surface can dry out slightly.

Keep an eye out for predators that can damage or destroy plants (especially in the earliest stages of growth). Prominent among these are slugs and snails, sowbugs, cutworms, and birds. Domestic pets, squirrels, and raccoons can be pests, too; they may find the soft, moist earth irresistible for digging.

## BROADCASTING SEEDS IN A PREPARED BED

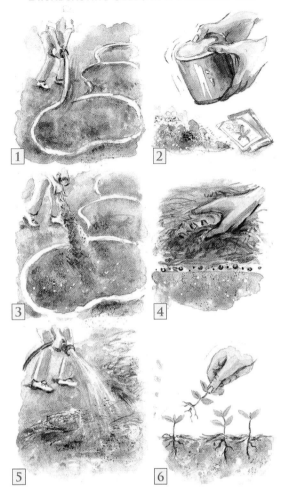

STEP 1: For a patterned planting, outline the areas for each kind of seed with gypsum, flour, or stakes and string. You may want to put a label in each area.

STEP 2: To achieve a more even distribution, shake each kind of seed in a covered can with several times its bulk of white sand.

STEP 3: Scatter the seed-sand mixture as evenly as possible over the bed or individual planting areas; then rake lightly, barely covering the seeds with soil. Take care not to bury them too deeply.

STEP 4: Spread a very thin layer of mulch (such as sifted compost) over the bed to help retain moisture, keep the surface from crusting, and hide the seeds from birds.

STEP 5: Water with a fine spray. Keep the soil surface barely damp until the seeds sprout; once seedlings have two or three sets of true leaves, gradually decrease watering frequency.

STEP 6: When seedlings have two sets of true leaves, thin those that are too closely spaced. If necessary, transplant the thinned seedlings to fill empty spaces in the bed.

## BARE-ROOT PLANTING

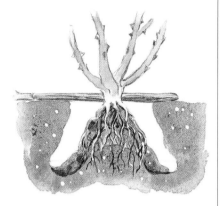

Dig hole to depth of roots. Make a firm cone of soil in center of hole; spread plant's roots over cone, positioning juncture of roots and stem at or slightly above soil grade (place a stick across hole to gauge plant's position). Fill in with soil; water well.

## PLANTING FROM LARGE CONTAINERS

Dig hole twice as wide as container and almost as deep; dig deeper around edges to give roots more room. (Central "plateau" of soil prevents settling after planting.) Remove plant from pot; loosen coiling or rootbound roots. Set plant in hole and fill in with soil; top of root ball will be an inch or two above grade. Water well.

## PLANTING FROM CONTAINERS

When you buy plants in containers, you save yourself the time and effort of raising plants to setting-out size: you just bring them home from the nursery and set them right into the beds you've prepared. You'll find annuals and perennials sold in a variety of containers, from cell-packs to 2- to 4-inch individual pots to gallon-size "cans." Shrubs are generally available in 1- to 5-gallon plastic containers. The illustrations at left and below show how to set out plants from large as well as small containers.

WHEN TO PLANT. Timing depends on the plants and your climate. If you're planting annuals, set out spring-flowering, cold-hardy types as early as possible: in winter in mild regions, in earliest spring (as soon as the soil can be worked) where winters are cold. Summer-blooming, frost-tender sorts can go out in early to midspring in mild climates, as soon as the danger of frost is past in colder areas.

Among perennials, spring-flowering kinds are usually planted in late summer or fall, summer- and fall-blooming ones in spring. Mail-order nurseries generally abide by that schedule, sending plants to you at the appropriate time. Container-grown perennials from retail nurseries can be planted at any time, though it's best to avoid the heat of summer; in cold-winter regions, you should also steer clear of late-fall planting, when early freezes are a danger. Whenever you set out plants, protect them from wind and intense sun for a time after planting. If possible, plant during cool, cloudy, calm weather.

## PLANTING BARE-ROOT PLANTS

A few perennials and some deciduous shrubs (notably roses) are sold during dormancy, as bare-root plants. Plant these as soon as possible after purchase, following the method shown in the illustration above left. As for container-grown plants, the objective is to position the juncture of stem and roots at or slightly above grade, with roots radiating outward and downward into the soil.

## PLANTING FROM SMALL CONTAINERS OR CELL-PACKS

STEP 1: Dig a hole for each plant, making it the same depth as the container and an inch or two wider.

STEP 2: With your fingers, lightly separate matted roots. If there's a pad of coiled white roots at the bottom of the pot, cut or pull it off so that new roots will form and grow into the soil.

STEP 3: Place each plant in its hole so that the top of the root ball is even with the soil surface. Firm soil around the roots; then water each plant with a gentle flow that won't disturb soil or roots.

# CARING FOR THE GARDEN

*Regular maintenance will keep your cutting garden looking good and blooming lavishly. You'll need to pay attention to watering, fertilizing, grooming, and pest control (including weed control).*

WATERING. To stay productive, most cutting-garden plants need regular watering: that is, the soil should be kept moist at the root zone, though it can dry out a little at the surface. In cool weather and in cool-summer areas, you may need to water only once a week or even less often; in warm to hot regions, the frequency may climb to two or even three times a week. Whatever your schedule, never let leaves, stems, or blossoms wilt before you water—keeping everything looking fresh is crucial when you're raising materials for cutting.

Recycled-rubber soaker hose

Where rainfall is normal during bloom time, overhead watering is inevitable. In general, though, plants stay in better condition if water is applied directly to the soil. This minimizes the need for staking tall plants and lessens the risk of damage to delicate petals or leaves. You can grow many cut flowers in vegetable garden–style rows, with irrigation furrows in between. There are, however, alternatives to this sort of system; two popular choices are drip irrigation and watering with soaker hoses. Either technique allows for layouts other than strict rows. With *drip irrigation,* you can—if you like—apply water to individual plants, choosing from a variety of emitter types that also deliver water at various rates (measured in gallons per hour). *Soaker hoses* ooze water evenly through a porous exterior; you need to snake them through a planting so they're positioned closely enough to give fairly even water distribution. Both soaker hoses and drip irrigation components are widely sold at hardware and home improvement stores. (For more information on drip irrigation, see *Sunset's Garden Watering Systems.*)

FERTILIZING. Nutrients keep plants growing actively, producing new leaves and blossoms. Your soil (especially after you've amended it) contains enough nutrients to get your plants off to a good start; supplemental fertilizer during the growing season will encourage steady, abundant growth and bloom.

*Fertilizer types and forms.* Among fertilizers, the simplest type is an all-purpose "complete" one, a product containing all three of the major nutrients: nitrogen (N), phosphorus (P), and potassium (K). The product label will note the percentage (by weight) of each nutrient the fertilizer contains, always presenting them in the N-P-K order. For example, an 8-10-10 product contains 8 percent nitrogen, 10 percent each phosphorus and potassium. Note that nitrogen is water-soluble and will be depleted over the course of a growing season, but the other two nutrients, once dug into the soil, will remain in place, available to roots, for a much longer period.

When it comes to fertilizer forms, your options can be bewildering. You'll find dry, granular kinds that go onto or into the soil and dissolve as plants are watered; you'll also see concentrates to be diluted in water and applied in liquid form. On top of these differences, there are natural (organic) and chemical (synthetic, inorganic) fertilizers. All are effective, but they do have some important differences.

## MULCHING

**Whatever your climate, mulching can help your garden. Spread in a 2- to 4-inch-thick layer over the soil, a mulch provides an insulating blanket. It slows the rate at which water evaporates from the soil, keeping soil (and roots) more evenly moist between waterings. In warm weather, it keeps soil cooler. It discourages the growth of weeds by blocking light from their seeds; in wet weather, it prevents mud from splashing up and dirtying blooms and foliage. The only time mulching is not a good idea is early in spring, when soil is still cool from the winter. At that time, growth will be better if soil can warm more rapidly, so wait to apply a mulch until later in the season, when weather and soil are warmer.**

**A good mulch should be readily permeable and, ideally, slow to decompose. All sorts of materials fill the bill nicely. Compost is a classic mulch, though it does decompose fairly quickly to become part of the soil beneath. Oak leaves and pine needles are other fine (and usually free) mulches, and they decay slowly. Various wood by-products can also serve as mulch; if you use these, make sure they're nitrogen fortified, so they won't compete with plant roots for nitrogen in the soil and in fertilizers.**

Derived from the remains of living organisms, *natural* fertilizers include blood meal, bone meal, and bat guano. Except for liquid types (fish emulsion, for example), they're slower to take effect than chemical products; they are best used at the soil-preparation stage, when nutrients need not be available immediately.

As the name implies, *chemical* fertilizers are manufactured from chemical sources (listed on the product label). On the whole, they're faster acting than natural kinds, but they do vary in just how quickly they deliver nutrients to plants. Among dry types, the fastest acting sorts contain nitrogen in the ammonia form (check the package label). If you're looking for slower, more sustained action, try a controlled-release kind. These fertilizers deliver nutrients over a longer period—from 3 to 9 months, depending on the brand. The granules are encapsulated in a permeable coating, and with each watering just a small amount of fertilizer leaches from the granule into the soil.

Whether natural or chemical, fertilizers applied in liquid form are the fastest acting of all, since the nutrients are already in solution. They offer an ultra-quick pick-me-up, but they also leach through the soil in a hurry. If you are using liquids, you may need to apply them more frequently than dry types during the bloom period, especially where the growing season is long.

*When to fertilize.* Work a complete fertilizer into the soil before setting out annuals and perennials; a 5-10-10 product is a good choice. This job is easy to do when you're preparing a new planting bed (see page 97). If you're setting out just a few plants in an existing bed, sprinkle a little fertilizer into each planting hole and work it in thoroughly, taking care that it does not come in contact with plant roots.

For most perennials, this initial fertilizing is adequate for the first year's growth. In the following years, feed annually in early spring, just as the plants start to grow. Use a nitrogen-only (or predominantly nitrogen) product, since nitrogen is the nutrient most needed when growth begins and the only one that will leach into the root zone.

For annuals, which put out quantities of flowers over a prolonged bloom period, you'll probably want to give periodic "boosters" as the season progresses. One application within a week after planting should carry annuals through the first half of their growing season. In cool-winter areas, give a second feeding after bloom begins, using a nitrogen fertilizer. Where winters are warmer and the growing season is longer, give supplemental feedings of nitrogen after flowering starts and again in late summer.

CONTROLLING PESTS, DISEASES, AND WEEDS. Pests are an unpleasant fact of gardening life—but one that must be faced, especially by the cut-flower grower aiming for healthy, blemish-free blossoms and foliage. Among chewing pests, snails and slugs are the most common; you can hand-pick and destroy them or put out poison baits (keep these away from pets and children). Other chewing pests include various worms and catepillars; hand-pick these as well, or use the biological control *Bt (Bacillus thuringiensis)*, which attacks only the pests and is nontoxic to nontarget creatures. Among sucking insects, aphids are ubiquitous. Fortunately, they come and go with some rapidity, and natural predators abound; a moderate infestation may need no control. However, you can combat them with water jets from the hose, insecticidal soap, or a natural pesticide containing pyrethrins.

Besides being unsightly, weeds growing among your chosen plants will compete for water and nutrients—reason enough to control them before they gain a foothold. Old-fashioned hand-pulling is still an effective control, and in beds designed for easy flower harvest, pulling weeds should be fairly simple as well. Mulching helps, too: applied at least 2 inches thick, a mulch effectively buries most weed seeds, blocking out light and preventing germination.

GROOMING. When you're growing flowers for cutting, you're not likely to have many dead blossoms to remove. But there's more to grooming than simple deadheading. You'll want to keep flowers in prime condition for picking, and that means doing a certain amount of staking and stabilizing so that stems remain upright. Plants with tall blossom stems and those with heavy flower loads (regardless of height) are the most likely to need extra support. The illustrations below show a variety of staking techniques.

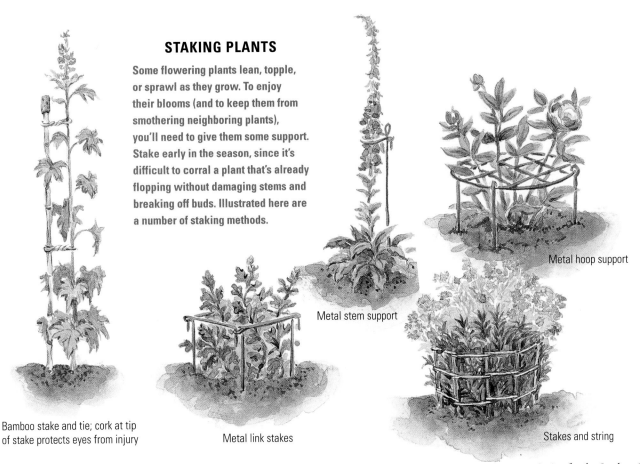

## STAKING PLANTS

Some flowering plants lean, topple, or sprawl as they grow. To enjoy their blooms (and to keep them from smothering neighboring plants), you'll need to give them some support. Stake early in the season, since it's difficult to corral a plant that's already flopping without damaging stems and breaking off buds. Illustrated here are a number of staking methods.

Bamboo stake and tie; cork at tip of stake protects eyes from injury

Metal link stakes

Metal stem support

Metal hoop support

Stakes and string

# HARVESTING AND CONDITIONING

*When you've spent time selecting just the right plants for your cutting garden, then nurtured them to their moment of glory, you don't want them to have a fleeting vase life. If you heed the following tips, your bouquets can easily avoid a premature trip to the compost heap.*

WHEN TO CUT. The best time to gather flowers and foliage is early in the morning, when plants have had the entire night to replenish the moisture and nutrients lost during the previous day. If you get to the job before the night's dew has evaporated, that's perfect! The second-best time to pick materials is early evening, when the sun has begun to set and plants are no longer stressed by bright sunlight and heat.

WHAT TO CUT. Outside in the garden, less-than-perfect flowers can put on a dazzling display—but for an arrangement, you want only the best. Look for unblemished flowers and foliage, free from pest and weather damage; cut only sturdy stems (unless spindly ones are the norm for the flower). To give yourself more flexibility in arranging your harvest, cut stems as long as you can without sacrificing the plant or reducing future flower production.

In general, blossoms should be picked on the youthful side of maturity, so they won't wilt or shatter soon after you've arranged them. A few exceptions are worth noting, however.

ฝ Some flowers, such as tulips, irises, and gladioli, are best gathered before fully open. In general, these are blooms with a fairly specific open-flower life (3 days for irises, for example).

ฝ Clustered blooms like lilacs or floribunda roses obviously can't be plucked with everything open and fresh at one time. Most arrangers prefer to cut these when the earliest buds have opened and others have yet to unfurl; they look more natural in the arrangement, and some of the unopened buds will unfold after cutting.

ฝ Certain flowers can shed copious amounts of pollen—lilies are a classic example. Pick these before pollen is shed and, if possible, remove the anthers before they release any.

HOW TO CUT. If cut flowers are to last well, their stems must retain the ability to take up moisture when put in water. For this reason, it's good practice to take a pail of tepid water with you into the garden so you can immerse cut stems at once, keeping their tissues turgid. This is not absolutely necessary, particularly if you're just dashing outside to cut a couple of stems, but it certainly helps maintain freshness if you're on a more far-ranging mission. Be sure your cutting tool—scissors, pruners, or knife—is sharp. Sharp tools make clean cuts, and clean cuts absorb water better.

## PROCESSING THE HARVEST

Once your cut material is indoors, recut the stems under water. Even if they were immersed in water immediately after cutting, there's a chance that the cutting process will have created a sort of "airlock" at the stem base—a barrier that will prevent the cut blossoms or foliage from absorbing water. Recutting the stem ends while they're submerged ensures free uptake of water. Make the cut at a 45-degree slant; this exposes more cells than a straight-across cut does, allowing for greater water absorption. A slanted cut also keeps stems from resting flush against the container's bottom. If you adjust stem lengths while composing an arrangement, recut under water each time.

SPECIAL STEM TREATMENTS. Certain types of stems should be recut or processed in a precise way to give them the longest life possible.

*Nodal stems.* These are stems like those of carnations, with a noticeable, swollen-looking "joint" where leaves attach. Make your cut above or below a node, but not directly through one.

*Stems from true bulb flowers.* When you cut a full-length flower stem from plants such as daffodils, tulips, and lilies, you'll see that the base is white and thicker than the green stem above it. Always make cuts into the green portion.

*Stems with milky sap.* Stems that exude a milky sap effectively seal themselves off when cut; water uptake is interrupted and flowers droop quickly. There are two ways to get around the problem. You can immerse the cut stem ends in boiling water for 30 seconds; or you can sear them with the flame from a match, candle, or gas burner. Euphorbia, hellebore, hollyhock, and poppy are examples of this group.

*Stems with clear sap.* Some cut stems bleed a clear sap that is slimy or slightly sticky; daffodils and callas are two familiar examples. Process these stems separately, apart from other flowers and from each other—daffodils separate from callas, for example. Place the cut stems in a tall container of water for several hours to let the clear gel bleed away. If you skip this step, the sap can foul the water in a bouquet, ruining all the other flowers.

*Hollow stems.* When you cut a hollow stem and place it in water, you create an air chamber in the hollow part. Wilting soon follows. Two treatments will remedy this. First, you can upend the stem and fill the hollow with water, then put your finger over the stem end and plunge it into the vase; this leaves the hollow core filled with water. This method is convenient only if the arrangement is simple—ideally, just the one stem! An easier approach is to upend the stem, fill it with water, and insert a cotton plug. The plug retains water long enough for you to place the stem easily in a vase, then acts as a wick to keep the hollow moist for the life of the arrangement. Delphiniums and lupines are two arrangers' favorites with hollow stems.

*Woody stems.* To enhance water-absorbing capacity, slit woody stems vertically for 1 to 2 inches up from the base; use hand pruners or a sharp knife. If the stems are especially thick—½ inch or more—a simple slit may not be enough. Instead, use a hammer to fracture the stem end.

## FINAL CONDITIONING

After you've cut and processed all stems, give them one last treatment before you place them in an arrangement. Remove foliage from parts of stems that will be beneath the water in the bouquet; if left on, it can begin to decay and foul the water. Then plunge the stems into cool water right up to flowers' necks and place in a cool, dim or dark place for several hours or overnight. During this time, they'll take up as much water as possible, becoming stiffer and better able to hold their positions when arranged.

### TULIP TIPS

Tulip stems are a special case—nice and straight on day one, they'll arch and twist by the second day, literally giving you a new twist on your original arrangement. If you want to discourage this behavior, you'll need to give them slightly different conditioning than that described in "Final Conditioning" (below left). Take a piece of paper (green florist's paper is good, but newspaper also works) and lay the tulip stems diagonally across it. Then roll up the tulips in the paper so stem ends protrude from one end of the resulting bundle, while blossoms are all held together (but not tightly) at the other end. Plunge the bundle into tepid water and keep in a cool, dark place for several hours to overnight.

A bucketful of freshly gathered roses awaits final cutting and arranging.

# ROSES

*A dozen long-stemmed red roses. What could be more classic—or classier? And if you think these beauties have to come from a florist, think again. By choosing the right varieties and giving the plants good care, you can grow your very own long-stemmed roses—in any color.*

'Paradise'

WHAT ROSES TO GROW. In truth, any rose is fair game for cutting and arranging, but some are better suited to the role than others. For good presentation, you want a flower with a stiff pedicel—the stalk at the top of the actual stem, immediately beneath the flower—so the blossom will remain upright or nearly so when placed in a bouquet. For the longest-lasting arrangement, you need a flower that won't rush from bud to open blossom in a matter of hours. Remember, too, that cluster-flowered roses rarely give the effect of a solid bunch of bloom; instead, the central flower usually opens before the surrounding buds do. If you cut when the central flower is perfect, the not-yet-open buds may or may not unfurl; if you cut when the surrounding buds are opening, the central flower is fading and must be removed for good appearance.

For all these reasons, the most popular roses for general cutting purposes are hybrid teas and grandifloras. These typically have long, strong stems and large blossoms that are borne individually or, in the case of grandifloras, in very small clusters. The best ones for cutting have petals with plenty of substance, and their flowers open slowly enough to hold an attractive shape for a number of days. Here are a number of proven cut-flower choices, presented by color.

TOP: 'Honor', 'Saint Patrick'
MIDDLE: 'Brandy,' 'Mister Lincoln'
BOTTOM: 'Sonia', 'Double Delight'

- ◌ WHITE. 'Crystalline', "Honor', 'Pascali'

- ◌ CREAM, YELLOW. 'Elina', 'Golden Masterpiece', 'Gold Medal', 'Saint Patrick'

- ◌ ORANGE, WARM BLENDS. 'Brandy', 'Fragrant Cloud', 'Just Joey', 'Medallion', 'Touch of Class'

- ◌ RED. 'Mister Lincoln', 'Olympiad', 'Toro'

- ◌ PINK. 'Bewitched', 'Bride's Dream', 'Fame!', 'Miss All-American Beauty', 'Perfume Delight', 'Queen Elizabeth', 'Royal Highness', 'Sonia'

- ◌ LAVENDER. 'Barbra Streisand', 'Lagerfeld', 'Paradise', 'Silverado'

- ◌ MULTICOLOR. 'Broadway', 'Double Delight', 'Peace'

ESSENTIAL ROSE CARE. To grow good roses, give the plants decent, well-drained soil, a sunny, preferably open location, regular water, and well-timed applications of fertilizer. You may also need to control pests and diseases, though this aspect of care is more of an issue in some climates—and in some rose varieties—than others.

The simplest way to give roses their preferred conditions is to grow them in a separate bed or beds. For ease of maintenance (and this includes cutting for arrangements), make the plantings just two bushes deep, so you can reach part of each bush from outside the bed. Planting in staggered rows makes access easiest. You can also grow roses in mixed cutting gardens, but if you elect to do this, choose the most vigorous, disease-resistant varieties available to you; they'll perform best under general garden conditions.

For more information on all aspects of rose care, consult the *Sunset* book *Roses*.

TIPS FOR CUTTING. Roses, like other flowers, are best cut in early morning or early evening (see "When to cut," page 106). Newly planted roses and those just getting established in the garden should not be heavily harvested; resist the urge to cut lots of blossoms and take long stems, since the plants need to retain as much foliage as possible to build up strength. When a plant is growing vigorously and blooming generously, however, you can cut a greater quantity of flowers with longer stems. Make cuts just above a leaf, preferably one pointing toward the outside of the plant; a new stem will spring from the growth bud at the leaf base. When you cut long stems, be sure the portion you leave on the plant has at least two sets of leaves.

Once you've brought your roses inside, recut and condition them as described on page 107. For ease of handling, some people remove all the thorns from each stem (there are even special stem strippers for the purpose), but this isn't necessary. For the longest possible vase life, recut the stems under water every other day, cutting each back by about ½ inch.

# LEAVES, BERRIES, AND BRANCHES

*Say it* without *flowers! Though the word "arrangement" is typically taken to mean "bouquet of flowers," other plant parts—leaves, berries, slender branches—also make lovely compositions. And of course, such materials also increase the beauty and variety of more traditional floral arrangements. Here's a selection of these invaluable non-blossoms.*

Hostas in variety

LEAVES Often striking enough to display on its own, foliage comes in a virtually infinite variety of sizes, shapes, even colors. Leaves from trees and shrubs are carried on woody stems, while those from perennials and some annuals have fleshy leafstalks more akin to flower stems—differences to bear in mind when you condition what you've gathered (see page 107). The plants listed here are all proven performers in arrangements, but they're by no means your only choices. Feel free to experiment: if you see foliage you like, cut it—then create!

**Trees.** *Eucalyptus* (evergreen): Especially the rounded silver gray leaves of *E. polyanthemos, E. pulverulenta. Magnolia grandiflora* (evergreen): Large, leathery, glossy oval leaves. *Prunus cerasifera* (cherry plum; deciduous): Purple-leafed selections such as 'Newport'.

**Shrubs, vines.** *Aucuba japonica* (Japanese aucuba; evergreen): Large, glossy, toothed leaves; many selections show white or yellow variegation. *Elaeagnus* (silverberry, Russian olive; evergreen and deciduous): Several species and named selections, some with silvery gray leaves, others variegated in white or yellow. *Euonymus* (evergreen species): Many selections with white or yellow variegation. *Hedera* (ivy; evergreen): English ivy is the most familiar of these vines, with many fancy-leafed forms as well as kinds variegated in white, yellow, silver. *Nandina domestica* (heavenly bamboo; evergreen): Big, elaborately divided leaves resemble those of bamboo, often turn red in winter.

**Perennials.** *Artemisia:* Various species with filigree foliage in silvery gray. *Asparagus* (ornamental): Filmy, fernlike foliage in sprays or wands. *Aspidistra elatior* (cast-iron plant): Lance-shaped, leathery, glossy leaves to 2 feet long. *Bergenia:* Big, glossy, rubbery, paddle-shaped leaves on long stalks. *Ferns:* Great number of species, some with feather-shaped fronds, others with sprays of small leaflets. *Hosta:* Amazing variation in leaf size (6 inches to 2 feet), shape (lancelike to round), and color (green, near-blue, blue gray, yellow, variegated). *Polygonatum* (Solomon's seal): Oval leaves ascend arching, 2- to 4-foot stems in ladder fashion. *Zantedeschia* (calla): Long-stalked, arrow-shaped leaves 1 to 1½ feet long; some kinds are white spotted.

**Annuals.** *Centaurea cineraria, Senecio cineraria* (dusty miller): Strap-shaped, many-lobed, woolly to velvety white leaves. *Coleus × hybridus:* Variegated leaves in countless color combinations featuring red, salmon, yellow, green, purple, white, cream. Some types have broadly oval leaves, others deeply lobed ones. *Euphorbia marginata* (snow-on-the-mountain): Oval green leaves margined and striped white. *Perilla frutescens purpurascens* (shiso): Oval, deeply toothed bronze to purple leaves.

BERRIES AND SEEDS A number of favorite flowering shrubs and vines also bear colorful berries. The fruit typically starts to color in late summer or early autumn, making it a staple for harvest-time and winter arrangements.

*Callicarpa* (beautyberry; deciduous): Graceful shrubs with arching branches bear clusters of shiny violet to rosy purple berries. *Celastrus* (bittersweet; deciduous): Vigorous twining vines with orange seed capsules that split to show red seeds. *Cotoneaster* (evergreen and deciduous): Clusters of red to red-orange berries on plants that vary from big, fountainlike shrubs to wide-spreading ground covers. *Euonymus:* Square "hatbox" fruits open to show red seeds. *E. fortunei* is an ever-green vine or shrub; *E. alatus, E. americanus,* and *E. europaeus* are deciduous shrubs. *Ilex* (holly; evergreen and deciduous): Shrubs and trees with spiny- or smooth-edged leaves; most have red berries, but a few bear creamy white or blue-black fruit. *Nandina domestica* (heavenly bam-boo; evergreen): Clumps of vertical stems bear feathery foliage and large, loose sprays of bright red berries. *Pyracantha* (firethorn; evergreen): Thorny shrubs of variable size with dense clusters of red, orange, or occasionally yellow berries. *Rosa* (rose; deciduous): Many cluster-flowering types bear sprays of small orange to red hips; *R. rugosa* has showy, cherry-size orange or red hips. *Viburnum* (deciduous and evergreen): Many deciduous species (such as *V. opulus,* European cranberry bush) bear clusters of red berries. Evergreen *V. davidii* and *V. tinus* have dark metallic blue fruit.

*Cornus stolonifera* (redtwig dogwood)

BRANCHES Bare stems have a strong, sculptural look, whether you present them on their own or use them as accents in mixed arrangements. Some have a striking shape, while others are valued for their vivid color.

**Elaborately twisted and contorted stems.** Possibilities include the following three deciduous shrubs to small trees: *Corylus avellana* 'Contorta' (Harry Lauder's walking stick), *Morus australis* 'Unryu' *(M. bombycis* 'Unryu'; contorted mulberry), and *Salix matsudana* 'Tortuosa' (corkscrew willow). Harvesting stems for arrangements does the plants no harm; the mulberry and willow, in fact, are vigorous enough to require repeated cutting back if they are to stay shrubby.

**Catkins.** Various so-called pussy willows are traditional harbingers of spring, their bare branches sporting velvety, furry catkins (actually the plants' male flowers). Choices include the following, all with 1- to 1½-inch catkins: *Salix caprea* (pinkish gray catkins); *S. discolor* (pearly gray); *S. gracilistyla* (gray catkins adorned with rose-and-gold anthers); *S. gracilistyla melanocalyx* (black with red anthers). Cut plants back heavily: it keeps them to a manageable size, and catkins come on new growth.

**Bright-colored stems.** Several shrubby dogwoods and willows share this feature. Among dogwoods are *Cornus alba* (bright red stems); *C. alba* 'Sibirica' (coral colored); *C. sanguinea* (dark red); *C. stolonifera* and several of its regional forms (bright red); and *C. stolonifera* 'Flaviramea' (chartreuse yellow). Willows include *Salix* 'Flame' and *S. alba* 'Britzensis', with vibrant red-orange stems; *S. alba vitellina* (brilliant yellow); and *S.* 'Golden Curls' (yellow, somewhat twisted). On all these shrubs, new growth is the most highly colored—so heavy annual pruning or harvesting produces plenty of material for the next year.

*Salix discolor* (pussy willow)

# CUT AND DRIED

*Have you ever wished your bouquets could last forever? Well, some can. If you start with the right flowers and seed heads and process them properly, you can craft arrangements that, if not literally everlasting, will remain fresh looking for months. Their only enemy is dust!*

The plants listed on these two pages can all be preserved by simple air drying. Begin by harvesting at the right moment: in the morning, after dew has dried but before temperatures climb. Keep different plants separate. Strip off any stem leaves, then gather the stems into bundles for drying; keep the bunches small, since crowding the stems hinders drying. Use a rubber band to hold the stems together; as they dry and shrink a bit, the band will hold the bundle tightly. Suspend the bundles upside down, separated from each anther, in a warm spot where air moves freely (good air circulation is crucial to successful drying). Depending on the plant, drying generally takes 1 to 3 weeks.

Some flowers and seed heads don't droop as they dry and can be dried successfully in an upright position. Such plants include very stiff types (the various "everlastings") as well as most ornamental grasses.

Certain flowers may droop a bit whether you dry them upside down or right side up; baby's breath and yarrow are good examples. For the most natural look, you can dry these upright, with their stems in a little water—just an inch or so in a fairly narrow container. This method lets the cut material dry very gradually, even more slowly than in air alone. Water not taken up by the stems will simply evaporate.

You'll find that many plants have easy-to-dry flowers and/or seed heads. A number of popular choices are presented below, divided according to plant type (annual or perennial). Note that this list is by no means exhaustive; you may well see other flowers in dried arrangements, and you should feel free to try drying blossoms other than those described here.

## ANNUALS

These plants complete their life cycle within 1 year. They usually sprout from seed in winter or spring, bloom during the warm months, and die before the year's end.

*Carthamus tinctorius.* Safflower. Orange-yellow, thistlelike blossoms come on 3-foot stems set with spiny-edged leaves.

*Celosia.* Cockscomb. Plume types are best for drying; they bear plumelike clusters of tiny flowers in bright yellow, orange, red, pink shades, and purple. Heights range from 1 to 3 feet.

*Consolida ajacis (C. ambigua).* Larkspur. Flowers like those of delphinium, in blue shades, white, pink, lilac, red; carried in 1- to 4-foot-high spikes.

*Gomphrena globosa.* Globe amaranth. Tight, cloverlike flower heads on branched stems 8 inches to 2 feet high; colors are white, lilac, purple, pink, rosy red.

*Grasses.* Annual grasses with attractive seed heads include *Briza maxima* (rattlesnake grass), *Coix lacryma-jobi* (Job's tears), *Lagurus ovatus* (hare's tail grass), and *Triticum turgidum,* Durum group (wheat).

*Helichrysum bracteatum.* Strawflower. Papery double daisies in white, yellow, orange, red, wine, and pink. Stems range from 1½ to 3 feet tall.

*Limonium sinuatum.* Statice. Winged stems 1½ to 2 feet high support clusters of small, cup-shaped, papery flowers in combinations of white with lavender, blue, pink, yellow, orange, purple.

*Lunaria annua.* Money plant. Ths is a biennial plant: it grows one year, flowers the next. Blossoms form decorative seed capsules that, when mature, look like translucent oval coins on widely branching stems to 3 feet high.

*Moluccella laevis.* Bells-of-Ireland. Upright stems to 3 feet bear tiered whorls of shell-shaped, crisp-textured apple green calyxes (the plant's "flowers").

*Nigella damascena.* Love-in-a-mist. Stems 1½ to 2 feet high bear blossoms in blue, white, or pink—but what arrangers gather are the balloonlike, horned seedpods.

*Scabiosa stellata.* Pincushion flower. Pale blue flowers bloom atop 1½-foot stems. After they fade, cup-shaped, tan to bronze bracts remain, packed into spherical heads that look like drumsticks (or exotic volleyballs).

## PERENNIALS

Where conditions are right for them, perennials will grow and flower year after year from an initial planting. General hardiness figures and any climate preferences are stated for each plant.

*Achillea filipendulina.* Fernleaf yarrow. Tiny yellow flowers in flat heads to 6 inches across are borne at the ends of 3- to 5-foot stems. Hardy to $-40°F/-40°C$.

*Astilbe.* False spiraea. Large, feathery plumes of tiny flowers appear above fernlike foliage. Plants range from 1½ to 5 feet high. Not for the Deep South. Hardy to $-30°F/-34°C$ (with snow cover).

*Catananche caerulea.* Cupid's dart. Threadlike stems to 3 feet tall; dark-centered blue or white daisies. Hardy to $-40°F/-40°C$.

*Echinops.* Globe thistle. Flower heads look like golf ball–size pincushions in metallic blue. Plants grow 2½ to 4 feet high. Hardy to $-40°F/-40°C$.

*Eryngium.* Sea holly. Unusual-looking flowers in steel blue, sea green, or near-gray consist of a dome-shaped flower head sitting on a ruff of spiky bracts. Heights run from 1½ to 4 feet. Most are hardy to $-20°F/-29°C$.

*Grasses.* Many perennial grasses furnish flower heads for drying—some feathery and plumelike, others more like foxtails or even slender bottlebrushes. Good choices include members of *Calamagrostis, Cortaderia, Miscanthus, Molinia, Panicum, Pennisetum, Rhynchelytrum, Stipa.* Size and hardiness vary; check with local nurseries for the best plants for your area.

*Gypsophila paniculata.* Baby's breath. Multibranched flower stems form a see-through cloud of ¼-inch white or pink blossoms. Named selections range from 1 to 4 feet tall. Hardy to $-35°F/-37°C$.

*Lavandula.* Lavender. Shrubby plants with thin stems topped in narrow clusters of tiny blue to violet blossoms. Many kinds exist; none likes hot, humid summers. English lavender *(L. angustifolia)* is hardy to $-20°F/-29°C$, lavandin *(L. × intermedia)* to $0°F/-18°C$. Other kinds are hardy to $15°F/-9°C$.

*Limonium gmelinii, L. perezii, L. platyphyllum (L. latifolium).* Statice. Many-branched flower stems produce broad heads of small, papery, typically blue flowers. *L. gmelinii* and *L. platyphyllum* are hardy to $-35°F/-37°C$. *L. perezii* is hardy only to $30°F/-1°C$ but can be grown as an annual in colder regions.

*Physalis alkakengi.* Chinese lantern. Starlike white summer flowers are followed in fall by papery orange seed husks reminiscent of Chinese lanterns. Plant is branching, to 3 feet high. Hardy to $0°F/-18°C$; can be grown as an annual in colder regions.

*Psylliostachys suworowii.* Leafless stems—some branched, some not—carry narrow, cylindrical spikes of tiny, papery lilac-pink flowers. Hardy to $-40°F/-40°C$.

## DRYING HYDRANGEAS

You can preserve hydrangea's lush, fluffy summertime flower heads to enjoy throughout the year. Most popular for drying are so-called mophead hydrangeas *(H. macrophylla),* but you also can use smooth, peegee, and oakleaf hydrangeas *(H. arborescens, H. paniculata* 'Grandiflora', and *H. quercifolia,* respectively). For best results, don't pick the flower heads at their richest color; wait until they're older and at least half the blossoms have turned greenish.

Once you have cut the stems and removed the foliage, you have two choices. You can hang the stems upside down in a cool, dark, airy place; the flower heads will wilt a bit while drying and be somewhat compact. For a more natural-looking result, slit the stem ends; then place the stems in a container holding about an inch of water. The stems will absorb some of the water, letting flowers dry very gradually; any excess water simply evaporates. After the water is gone, suspend the largely dried flowers upside down in a cool, dark, airy place until totally dry. Colored flowers do not retain their original hues, but instead dry largely to beige and tan tones.

# Plans for Cutting Gardens

*Once you have the basic knowledge you need to establish plots of plants for cutting, it's time for the the fun part— creating the actual garden! For inspiration, look to these 12 pages, offering 11 plans for various times of year and garden situations.*

*Each planting scheme is accompanied by a color illustration, showing the garden at its peak, and a plot plan with each plant shaded in the basic color of its flowers (or foliage) and labeled by a letter. These letters identify the plants for you: just find the corresponding letter in the plant list provided. For every plant in the list, we give botanical name and common name (if there is one); the number in parentheses indicates the total number of that plant used in the garden shown. For details on how to read these plans, check the example below (taken from page 120).*

**PLAN ILLUSTRATION AND DESCRIPTION**

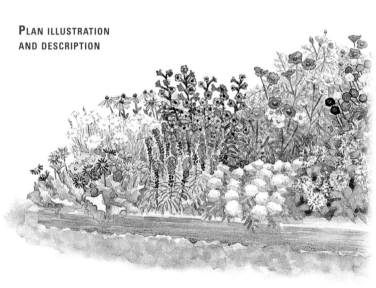

**PLANT LIST** — Botanical name

**A. Penstemon × gloxinioides 'Garnet'.**
Border penstemon (2) — Common name

**B. Liatris spicata 'Kobold'.**
Gayfeather (3)

**C. Chrysanthemum maximum 'Esther Read'.**
Shasta daisy (4)

**D. Echinacea purpurea 'Bravado'.** — Cultivar name
Purple coneflower (2)

**E. Gerbera jamesonii.**
Transvaal daisy (6) — Number of plants used in plan

**F. Veronica spicata 'Icicle'.**
Speedwell (3)

**G. Coreopsis rosea (4)**

**H. Gladiolus, Grandiflora hybrid, light yellow cultivar (8)**

**I. Cosmos bipinnatus, Versailles strain (6)**

Letter corresponds to plant location in plot plan

**PLOT PLAN**

Dimensions of planting — Planting area: 16' x 6'

## Summer Flower Factory

Railroad ties enclose a 6- by 16-foot cutting garden designed for pure efficiency. Over half the plants used here are brilliant annuals. Where winter temperatures dip to 15°F/−9°C, you'll also need to grow the Transvaal daisy (E) as an annual, replacing it every year; where lows fall below 10°F/−12°C, replace the border penstemon (A) with *P. digitalis*. The other plants, though, will flourish in frostless regions as well as in climates with winter temperatures as low as −20°F/−29°C. And if you replace *Coreopsis rosea* (G) with *Chrysanthemum × rubellum* 'Clara Curtis', the range for most extends to areas with lows down to −30°F/−34°C.

# SPRINGTIME FLOWER FACTORY

This planting looks lush, perhaps even a bit wild—but its exuberance disguises a hard-working and efficient setup. The planting area (6 feet deep and 14 feet long) packs a floral wallop in an easy-to-harvest layout. Plants A through G are perennials and bulbs which can be expected to persist for several to many years and will take winter temperatures as low as −30°F/−34°C.

Where winters are nearly frost-free, choose a peony (A) with Japanese flower form: these need the least winter chill. The tulips (H) may need annual replacing in warmer-winter regions. The anemones (I) must be dug and stored over winter where lows regularly dip below 0°F/−18°C; the freesias (J) need digging and storage below 20°F/−7°C.

## PLANT LIST

**A.** Paeonia, herbaceous hybrid (e.g. 'Festiva Maxima'). Peony (1)

**B.** Iris, tall bearded cultivar (e.g. 'Silverado', 'Beverly Sills') (6)

**C.** Aquilegia, McKana Giants strain. Columbine (8)

**D.** Dianthus caryophyllus. Border carnation (6)

**E.** Iberis sempervirens. Evergreen candytuft (4)

**F.** Primula × polyantha. Polyanthus primrose (4)

**G.** Narcissus, trumpet or large-cupped cultivar (e.g. 'Mount Hood', 'Ice Follies'). Daffodil (5)

**H.** Tulipa, mixed Single Late types. Tulip (8)

**I.** Anemone coronaria. Poppy-flowered anemone (9)

**J.** Freesia, Tecolote hybrid (6)

**K.** Consolida ajacis, Steeplechase strain. Larkspur (5)

**L.** Antirrhinum majus, Rocket strain. Snapdragon (8)

**M.** Centaurea cyanus, Polka Dot strain. Bachelor's button (8)

**N.** Viola × wittrockiana. Pansy (6)

**O.** Viola cornuta. Viola (4)

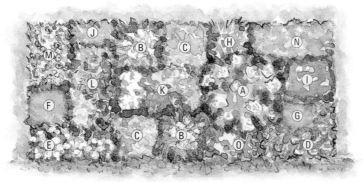

Planting area: 14' x 6'

# SPRING BORDER 1

Dress up a blank wall with a cheery spring border that just happens to be a cutting garden, too. Anchored by a mock orange (A) and a climbing rose (B), five perennials and six annuals put on a bright and varied show. The plants in this garden all perform best with some winter chill, be it fairly light (regular frosty nights, for example) to quite severe (lows to −30°F/−34°C or a bit lower). In the colder areas, where temperatures regularly drop to 0°F/−18°C or below, you'll need to protect the rose over the winter. The coral bells (I) and evergreen candytuft (L) will appreciate a winter mulch if snow cover fails.

## PLANT LIST

**A.** Philadelphus × virginalis 'Glacier'. Mock orange (1)

**B.** Rosa 'Constance Spry'. Climbing rose (1)

**C.** Paeonia (herbaceous), cherry red cultivar. Peony (2)

**D.** Iris, Siberian, 'White Swirl' or other white cultivar (2)

**E.** Chrysanthemum coccineum. Painted daisy (2)

**F.** Nigella damascena, Persian Jewels strain. Love-in-a-mist (8)

**G.** Antirrhinum majus, Rocket or Topper strain. Snapdragon (10)

**H.** Papaver nudicaule. Iceland poppy (9)

**I.** Heuchera sanguinea. Coral bells (5)

**J.** Calendula officinalis, cream-colored cultivar (3)

**K.** Viola × wittrockiana. Pansy (5)

**L.** Iberis sempervirens. Evergreen candytuft (3)

**M.** Consolida ajacis, Steeplechase strain. Larkspur (4)

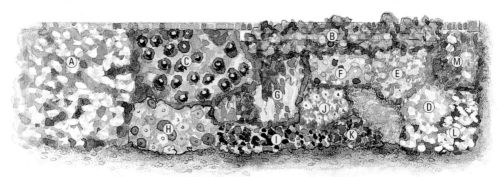

Planting area: 20' x 5'

# SPRING BORDER 2

It uses the same setting and layout as the plan on the facing page, but this second spring border will thrive in mild-winter regions—though the plants can take lows in the −10 to −20°F/−23 to −29°C range. The anchors are a European cranberry bush (A), which provides an autumn bonus of colorful fruits, and a climbing rose (B) that's also noted for its fall display of large, showy hips. If winter temperatures do regularly fall to 10°F/ −12°C or lower, protect the rose over winter, and dig and store the Persian ranunculus (H).

## PLANT LIST

**A.** Viburnum opulus 'Compactum'. European cranberry bush (1)

**B.** Rosa 'Mme. Grégoire Staechelin'. Climbing rose (1)

**C.** Centranthus ruber, red form. Jupiter's beard (2)

**D.** Iris, tall bearded, light yellow cultivar (2)

**E.** Euphorbia amygdaloides 'Purpurea' (3)

**F.** Clarkia unguiculata, Royal Bouquet strain. Mountain garland (8)

**G.** Antirrhinum majus, Cinderella strain. Snapdragon (10)

**H.** Ranunculus asiaticus. Persian ranunculus (9)

**I.** Aquilegia, Music strain. Columbine (6)

**J.** Lathyrus odoratus, Supersnoop strain. Bush sweet pea (3)

**K.** Dianthus plumarius. Cottage pink (3)

**L.** Iberis sempervirens. Evergreen candytuft (3)

**M.** Digitalis grandiflora. Yellow foxglove (4)

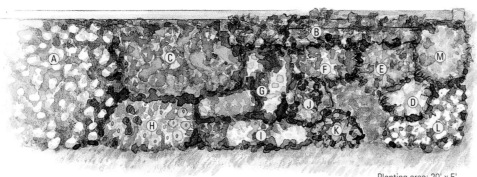

Planting area: 20' x 5'

# SUMMER ISLAND 1

Surrounded by lawn, this flowery island offers a dazzling array of pickables that will give you bouquets all summer long. With regular watering, the plants will grow in a wide range of climates: they'll flourish in frost-free regions but take lows of −20°F/−29°C, as well. To make the planting suitable for even colder areas—where temperatures dip to −40°F/−40°C—replace *Coreopsis rosea* (J) with *Chrysanthemum × rubellum* 'Clara Curtis'. (Note, however, that you'll need to dig and store the dahlias over winter in any climate.) By drawing a line between the arrows at either end of the bed, you can separate the planting into two pieces, either of which can be used against a fence, wall, or house.

## PLANT LIST

**A.** Dahlia, bright yellow ball or pompon type (2)

**B.** Gypsophila paniculata. Baby's breath (2)

**C.** Chrysanthemum maximum. Shasta daisy (8)

**D.** Alcea rosea, Chater's Double strain, pale yellow cultivar. Hollyhock (4)

**E.** Phlox maculata 'Alpha'. Thick-leaf phlox (3)

**F.** Physostegia virginiana 'Variegata'. False dragonhead (2)

**G.** Achillea 'Moonshine'. Yarrow (4)

**H.** Echinacea purpurea 'Bravado'. Purple coneflower (3)

**I.** Liatris spicata 'Silvertips'. Gayfeather (1)

**J.** Coreopsis rosea (2)

**K.** Veronica spicata 'Rotfuchs' ('Red Fox'). Speedwell (4)

**L.** Alchemilla mollis. Lady's-mantle (2)

**M.** Salvia splendens, purple selection. Scarlet sage (7)

**N.** Nicotiana alata, Nicki strain. Flowering tobacco (18)

**O.** Tagetes erecta, Sweet Cream strain. African marigold (9)

**P.** Silene coeli-rosa. Viscaria (5)

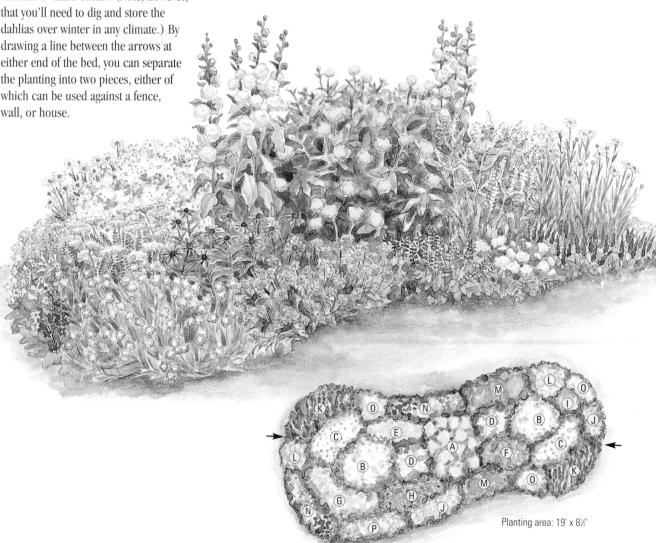

Planting area: 19' x 8½'

## PLANT LIST

**A.** **Buddleja davidii 'Harlequin'.** Butterfly bush (1)

**B.** **Baptisia australis.** Blue false indigo (1)

**C.** **Centranthus ruber 'Albus'.** Jupiter's beard (5)

**D.** **Artemisia ludoviciana 'Silver King'** (2)

**E.** **Asclepias tuberosa 'Hello Yellow'.** Butterfly weed (4)

**F.** **Achillea filipendulina 'Coronation Gold'.** Fernleaf yarrow (9)

**G.** **Penstemon barbatus** (3)

**H.** **Carthamus tinctorius (spineless form).** Safflower (6)

**I.** **Crocosmia 'Solfatare'** (6)

**J.** **Coreopsis lanceolata** (10)

**K.** **Limonium perezii.** Statice (5)

**L.** **Cosmos bipinnatus, Sonata series** (12)

**M.** **Gaillardia pulchella 'Red Plume'.** Blanket flower (7)

**N.** **Celosia 'Apricot Brandy'.** Plume cockscomb (9)

**O.** **Rudbeckia hirta 'Sonora'.** Gloriosa daisy (5)

# SUMMER ISLAND 2

If you live where water is in short supply and summers are warm to hot, this island planting is for you: it keeps the cut flowers coming with just moderate watering. Like the planting on the facing page, it's agreeable to a variety of climates, thriving where there's virtually no frost as well as in regions where winter temperatures fall to −20°F/−29°C. Where lows regularly dip to 0°F/−18°C or below, dig and store the crocosmia (I) over winter. Statice (K) will be perennial only in the mildest regions; for a hardy perennial substitute, choose *Limonium platyphyllum (L. latifolium)*. Like Summer Island 1, this planting can be separated into two beds, either suitable for planting against a wall or fence; just draw a line connecting the arrows on either end of the bed.

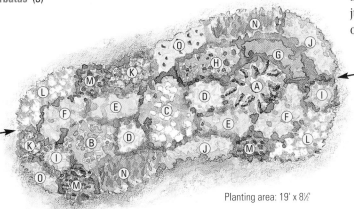

Planting area: 19' x 8½'

# SUMMER FLOWER FACTORY

Railroad ties enclose a 6- by 16-foot cutting garden designed for pure efficiency. Over half the plants used here are brilliant annuals. Where winter temperatures dip to 15°F/−9°C, you'll also need to grow the Transvaal daisy (E) as an annual, replacing it every year; where lows fall below 10°F/−12°C, replace the border penstemon (A) with *P. digitalis*. The other plants, though, will flourish in frostless regions as well as in climates with winter temperatures as low as −20°F/−29°C. And if you replace *Coreopsis rosea* (G) with *Chrysanthemum × rubellum* 'Clara Curtis', the range for most extends to areas with lows down to −30°F/−34°C.

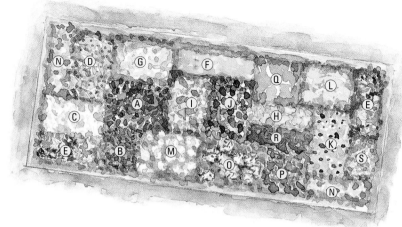

Planting area: 16' x 6'

## PLANT LIST

**A.** Penstemon × gloxinioides 'Garnet'. Border penstemon (2)

**B.** Liatris spicata 'Kobold'. Gayfeather (3)

**C.** Chrysanthemum maximum 'Esther Read'. Shasta daisy (4)

**D.** Echinacea purpurea 'Bravado'. Purple coneflower (2)

**E.** Gerbera jamesonii. Transvaal daisy (6)

**F.** Veronica spicata 'Icicle'. Speedwell (3)

**G.** Coreopsis rosea (4)

**H.** Gladiolus, Grandiflora hybrid, light yellow cultivar (8)

**I.** Cosmos bipinnatus, Versailles strain (6)

**J.** Scabiosa atropurpurea, Double Mixed strain. Pincushion flower (8)

**K.** Rudbeckia hirta 'Marmalade'. Gloriosa daisy (6)

**L.** Tagetes erecta, Perfection strain. African marigold (6)

**M.** Tagetes erecta, Sweet Cream strain. African marigold (6)

**N.** Tagetes patula. French marigold (10)

**O.** Zinnia elegans 'Candy Stripe' (8)

**P.** Limonium sinuatum. Statice (6)

**Q.** Nicotiana alata, Nicki strain. Flowering tobacco (6)

**R.** Perilla frutescens. Shiso (3)

**S.** Gypsophila elegans. Annual baby's breath (3)

# A PLANTING FOR FALL

Warm blossom colors and the tawny seed heads of grasses give this planting an unmistakable harvest-time aura: the flowers just beg to be cut and arranged in centerpieces with pumpkins, pomegranates, and other autumn bounty. And if you cut and dry the grasses, you'll have material for arrangements in seasons to come. New York and Italian asters (D and E) provide brilliant blue counterpoints to the golds, reds, and oranges of the other flowers. This planting is a largely permanent one; only the final four plants (J through M) need annual removal and replacement. And all the perennials adapt to a wide range of climates, thriving in virtually frostless areas as well as those where winter lows dip to −20°F/−29°C.

## PLANT LIST

**A.** **Calamagrostis × acutiflora 'Karl Foerster'.** Feather reed grass (2)

**B.** **Panicum virgatum 'Heavy Metal'.** Switch grass (1)

**C.** **Solidago 'Goldenmosa'.** Goldenrod (2)

**D.** **Aster novi-belgii 'Marie Ballard'.** New York aster (3)

**E.** **Aster amellus.** Italian aster (4)

**F.** **Sedum 'Autumn Joy'** (3)

**G.** **Helenium 'Crimson Beauty'.** Sneezeweed (2)

**H.** **Chrysanthemum × morifolium, cream or light yellow cushion type.** Florists' chrysanthemum (7)

**I.** **Gaillardia × grandiflora 'Goblin Yellow'** (3)

**J.** **Tithonia rotundifolia.** Mexican sunflower (6)

**K.** **Helianthus annuus 'Prado Red'.** Annual sunflower (4)

**L.** **Celosia 'Apricot Brandy'.** Plume cockscomb (5)

**M.** **Tagetes patula.** French marigold (12)

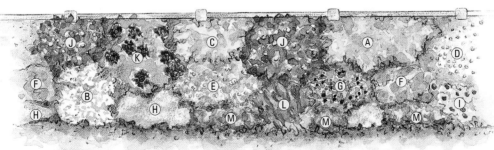

Planting area: 20' x 5'

# THREE-SEASON GARDEN 1

A varied assortment of annuals, perennials, and one red rose keeps the bouquets coming from spring to frost. Not everything will be flowering at once, of course, but even the out-of-bloom plants present an attractively leafy appearance. This planting needs a bit of winter chill and takes lows of −10 to −20°F/−23 to −29°C. By substituting *Chrysanthemum × rubellum* 'Clara Curtis' for *Coreopsis rosea* (L) and *Aster novae-angliae* 'Andenken an Alma Pötschke' ('Alma Pötschke') for *Aster × frikartii* 'Mönch' (M), you can enjoy the garden in even colder areas, where lows dip to −30 to −40°F/−34 to −40°C. Where winter temperatures consistently drop to 10°F/−12°C or lower, the 'Mister Lincoln' rose (A) will need protection.

## PLANT LIST

A. **Rosa 'Mister Lincoln'.** Hybrid tea rose (1)

B. **Gypsophila paniculata.** Baby's breath (2)

C. **Paeonia (herbaceous), pink cultivar.** Peony (1)

D. **Chrysanthemum maximum.** Shasta daisy (3)

E. **Alcea rosea, Chater's Double strain.** Hollyhock (6)

F. **Physostegia virginiana 'Variegata'.** False dragonhead (1)

G. **Psylliostachys suworowii** (3)

H. **Aquilegia, Music strain.** Columbine (2)

I. **Scabiosa caucasica.** Pincushion flower (3)

J. **Heuchera sanguinea.** Coral bells (2)

K. **Iberis sempervirens 'Autumn Snow'.** Evergreen candytuft (3)

L. **Coreopsis rosea** (3)

M. **Aster × frikartii 'Mönch'** (2)

N. **Zinnia elegans 'Candy Stripe'** (4)

O. **Antirrhinum majus, Rocket or Topper strain.** Snapdragon (4)

P. **Cosmos bipinnatus 'Picotee'** (6)

Q. **Nicotiana alata, Domino strain.** Flowering tobacco (6)

R. **Tagetes erecta, Sweet Cream strain.** African marigold (6)

S. **Viola × wittrockiana.** Pansy (3)

T. **Gomphrena globosa.** Globe amaranth (5)

Planting area: 9' x 20'

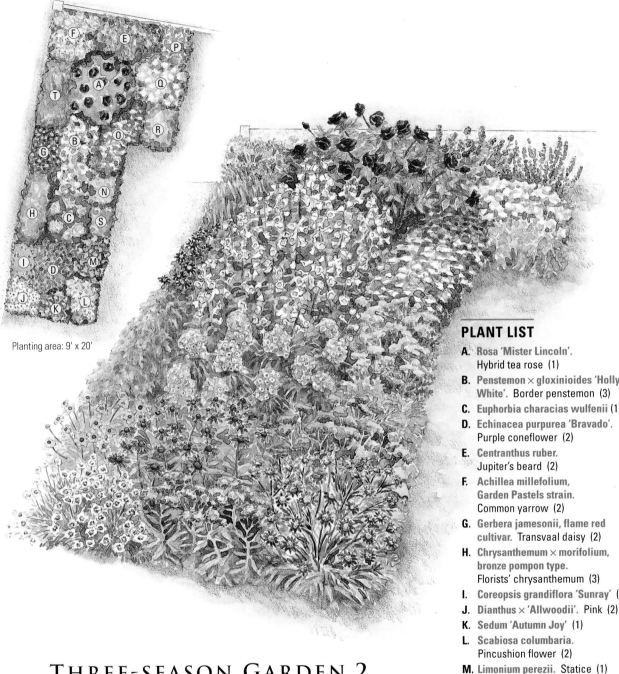

Planting area: 9' x 20'

# THREE-SEASON GARDEN 2

In design, this planting is a mirror image of Three-season Garden 1 (facing page), but in choice of plants, it's not the same at all. The 'Mister Lincoln' rose (A) is a common element (what's a complete cutting garden without a red rose?), but nearly all else is different, selected to suit warmer-winter climates. Though about a third of the plants will survive subzero winters, the group as a whole does best where temperatures normally remain above 10°F/−12°C. The Transvaal daisy (G) is hardy only to 15°F/−9°C; the statice (M) is perennial only in frostless and nearly frost-free climes.

## PLANT LIST

**A.** **Rosa 'Mister Lincoln'.** Hybrid tea rose (1)

**B.** **Penstemon × gloxinioides 'Holly's White'.** Border penstemon (3)

**C.** **Euphorbia characias wulfenii** (1)

**D.** **Echinacea purpurea 'Bravado'.** Purple coneflower (2)

**E.** **Centranthus ruber.** Jupiter's beard (2)

**F.** **Achillea millefolium, Garden Pastels strain.** Common yarrow (2)

**G.** **Gerbera jamesonii, flame red cultivar.** Transvaal daisy (2)

**H.** **Chrysanthemum × morifolium, bronze pompon type.** Florists' chrysanthemum (3)

**I.** **Coreopsis grandiflora 'Sunray'** (2)

**J.** **Dianthus × 'Allwoodii'.** Pink (2)

**K.** **Sedum 'Autumn Joy'** (1)

**L.** **Scabiosa columbaria.** Pincushion flower (2)

**M.** **Limonium perezii.** Statice (1)

**N.** **Achillea × taygetea.** Yarrow (2)

**O.** **Iberis sempervirens 'Autumn Snow'.** Evergreen candytuft (3)

**P.** **Linaria purpurea.** Toadflax (4)

**Q.** **Tagetes erecta, Sweet Cream strain.** African marigold (4)

**R.** **Calendula officinalis, cream-colored cultivar** (2)

**S.** **Papaver nudicaule.** Iceland poppy (2)

**T.** **Celosia 'Apricot Brandy'.** Plume cockscomb (4)

# A GARDEN FOR WINTER

Only fortunate gardeners in the West and parts of the South and Southeast can grow a cutting garden for winter arrangements. Even in these favored regions, though, choices are limited to those few plants that normally bloom in winter—and to early-spring bloomers that will flower in winter where chill is slight. The planting illustrated above, hardy to about 0°F/−18°C, offers an assortment suited to the cooler parts of winter-bloom territory, regions where cool days and frosty nights are the norm. The alternate plant assortment is almost as hardy, but it thrives where winter days are warm and frost is light or absent.

## PLANT LIST FOR COOLER REGIONS

**A.** **Camellia japonica 'Kramer's Supreme'** (1)

**B.** **Corylus avellana 'Contorta'.** Harry Lauder's walking stick (1)

**C.** **Chaenomeles 'Jet Trail'.** Flowering quince (1)

**D.** **Viburnum opulus 'Compactum'.** European cranberry bush (1)

**E.** **Erica carnea 'Vivellii'.** Heath (2)

**F.** **Erica carnea 'Winter Beauty'.** Heath (4)

**G.** **Helleborus orientalis.** Lenten rose (6)

**H.** **Bergenia crassifolia.** Winter-blooming bergenia (3)

**I.** **Primula × polyantha.** Polyanthus primrose (10)

**J.** **Viola odorata.** Sweet violet (8)

## PLANT LIST FOR WARMER REGIONS

**A.** **Camellia japonica 'Debutante'** (1)

**B.** **Viburnum tinus 'Spring Bouquet'.** Laurustinus (1)

**C.** **Chaenomeles 'Texas Scarlet'.** Flowering quince (1)

**D.** **Nandina domestica 'Gulf Stream'.** Heavenly bamboo (3)

**E.** **Papaver nudicaule.** Iceland poppy (10)

**F.** **Helleborus orientalis.** Lenten rose (8)

**G.** **Rhododendron (azalea), white-flowered cultivar (e.g. 'Everest', 'Glacier', 'Madonna')** (2)

**H.** **Euphorbia × martinii** (5)

**I.** **Calendula officinalis, cream-colored cultivar** (10)

**J.** **Viola × wittrockiana.** Pansy (18)

Planting area: 25' x 8'

## SPRING

**A. Clarkia amoena.**
Farewell-to-spring (3)

**B. Antirrhinum majus, Ribbon series.**
Snapdragon (3)

**C. Consolida ajacis.** Larkspur (3)

**D. Papaver nudicaule, Champagne
Bubbles strain.** Iceland poppy (4)

**E. Calendula officinalis,
cream-colored cultivar** (2)

**F. Viola × wittrockiana.**
Pansy (7)

**G. Primula × polyantha.**
Polyanthus primrose (5)

**H. Dianthus caryophyllus.**
Border carnation (2)

# A CONTAINER GARDEN

A cutting garden can be as close as your deck or patio—all you need is an assortment of containers and a few suitable plants. You have a variety of choices for each season; we show two possible groupings, one for spring and another for summer. In practice, though, you'll probably want to plant both spring and summer bloomers in order to get the longest possible display from your available space. To accommodate the larger plants, half-barrels are the simplest containers to use, since they hold a large volume of soil. But even the other containers are fairly sizable: none is less than 1 foot across or shallower than 8 inches.

## SUMMER

**I. Cosmos bipinnatus, Sonata series** (4)

**J. Rudbeckia hirta 'Marmalade'.**
Gloriosa daisy (3)

**K. Scabiosa atropurpurea.**
Pincushion flower (4)

**L. Gerbera jamesonii,
cream-colored cultivar.**
Transvaal daisy (2)

**M. Verbena 'Homestead Purple'** (1)

**N. Coreopsis grandiflora 'Sunray'** (7)

**O. Tagetes patula.**
French marigold (5)

**P. Limonium perezii.**
Statice (1)

# INDEX

Page Numbers in **boldface** refer to photographs.